The United Kingdom in the United Nations

Presented to Parliament
by the Secretary of State for Foreign and Commonwealth Affairs
by Command of Her Majesty
September 2003

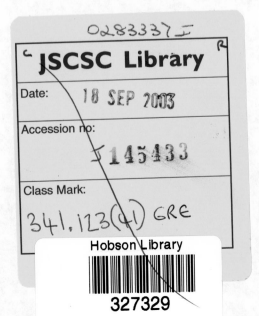

Cm 5898

£10.50

PREFACE BY THE FOREIGN SECRETARY

Though the United Nations is rarely out of the news, too little is known about all that it does, and of the United Kingdom's important contribution to its work. With the UK assuming the Presidency of the Security Council this month, and the new September Parliamentary Session and the General Assembly later this month, I decided earlier in the summer that there should be an annual report to Parliament about "the United Kingdom in the United Nations". This is the first edition – because of this it necessarily involves more background and history than subsequent reports will need to include.

During my period as Foreign Secretary, the work of the Security Council and of many agencies has been dominated by the shock waves caused by the world's worst ever terrorist outrage on 11th September 2001. Mostly there is agreement about what to do next; sometimes – as on Iraq earlier this year – there is not. But always the UN is relevant, key to the peaceful resolution of conflict. And I have in this period been able to witness the inspired leadership of Kofi Annan, UN Secretary-General, and the high professionalism of his staff.

Whilst so many have lost their lives as victims of terrorism, many of us I think imagined that the UN – the world's agency for peace – might at least not be targeted. That belief was, however, rudely shattered on August 19th, when a huge bomb at the UN Headquarters in Baghdad killed 22, injured over 100, and led to a scaling down of all work by humanitarian agencies in Iraq. Amongst the victims was Sergio Vieira de Mello, the Secretary-General's Personal Representative and the High Commissioner for Human Rights, a most distinguished international public servant, and one Briton, Fiona Watson, serving as a political affairs officer, and known personally to many members of the Commons for her work as a Researcher in the International Section of the Library. We mourn the loss of Mr de Mello, Miss Watson and all those others who perished on 19th August, and salute their dedication and courage. Never has the UN been more needed.

Jack Straw
Secretary of State for Foreign & Commonwealth Affairs

September 2003

I INTRODUCTION

1. This command paper describes the full range of the United Nations' activities and the United Kingdom's involvement in them. It briefly surveys the UK's contribution to the UN over the 58 years of the organisation's history. And it concludes by setting out a vision for UN reform in the future (Part IV). The paper will demonstrate three themes. Firstly, the United Nations is an enormously varied and active organisation across almost all fields of human endeavour: political, economic, social, human rights, environmental, medical and even meteorological. Secondly, the UK is and has always been a very active member of the organisation. With France, we are the only major power to have been a member of both the League of Nations (the UN's pre-war predecessor) and the United Nations throughout the entire history of those two organisations. Thirdly, the UN is a dynamic and constantly changing organisation, which has adapted remarkably well to meet the changes in the world since its foundations in 1945 and which needs to continue to change if it is to remain healthy and dynamic for the foreseeable future.

2. The United Kingdom played a critical role in the creation of the United Nations. It was discussions between Winston Churchill and Franklin Roosevelt aboard HMS Prince of Wales and USS Augusta in August 1941 that produced the Atlantic Charter, the first set of principles outlining a shape for the post-war order. British, American and Soviet representatives held the Dumbarton Oaks conversations three years later, at which most of the core elements of the United Nations organisation were agreed. And British ministers and diplomats again occupied central positions in the negotiations at the San Francisco Conference in April 1945, at which the United Nations Charter was signed. The United Nations that emerged accorded closely with British desires for an organisation strong and inclusive enough to provide order, yet flexible and realistic in the face of existing power realities.

3. The aims of the UN, as defined in 1945, include the maintenance of international peace and security, a reaffirmation of faith in fundamental human rights, the establishment of conditions for justice and international law and the promotion of economic and social development. These aims sit well with UK priorities today – security, prosperity and a better quality of life world-wide. Self-evidently, the delivery of these aims requires a system of global governance, such as only the UN provides. And today, as the pace of globalisation increases, the UN is more relevant and necessary than ever as a means of resolving the global challenges that face humanity. Growing international communication and inter-dependence, creating both opportunities and frustrations, produce an ever more pressing need for an international organisation that provides effective institutions of global governance, encourages productive exchanges between nations and seeks to ensure that the benefits of globalisation are widely shared.

4. The first meetings of the United Nations were held in London, before its move to New York. The first session of the General Assembly was held in Central Hall Westminster on 10 January 1946. With British diplomat Gladwyn Jebb (later Lord Gladwyn) acting as Secretary-General the United Nations was duly inaugurated, and the first General Assembly President and Secretary-General elected. One week later the Security Council met for the first time, in Church House, Westminster, with the Soviet presence in Iran immediately on the agenda. In 1947 two dedicated divisions were set up within the Foreign Office to handle United Nations issues, covering political and economic aspects respectively.

5. The United Kingdom has always been a major contributor to the United Nations and its agencies. The British influence on the founding of the United Nations Agencies was profound. As a Permanent Member of the Security Council, the UK was largely excluded from participation in peacekeeping during the Cold War. But we made a major contribution to the United Nations force in Cyprus, and as early as the 1960s British policymakers were calling for an expansion in the quantity and scope of peacekeeping missions. This took concrete shape after the Cold War, with the United Kingdom playing a significant role in the evolution of a peacekeeping doctrine in New York and deploying troops to United Nations and UN-mandated missions in Africa, the Balkans and elsewhere.

6. The United Kingdom has been a key player in the development of the United Nations human rights system. British proposals for the language setting out the United Nations purposes and principles were incorporated into Article 1 of the Charter with little change. The United Kingdom then played an important role in the drafting of the Universal Declaration of Human Rights, voted for it when it came before the General Assembly in December 1948, and continued to play a prominent role in putting the rights set out in the Declaration into legal form. The UK also played a significant role in the drafting of the International Covenant on Civil and Political Rights, and the International Covenant on Economic, Social and Cultural Rights. By 1991 the United Kingdom had ratified all six major international human rights instruments. British involvement in applying and developing an international criminal justice system has spanned the United Nations era from the British judges presiding over the first international war crimes tribunal at Nuremberg in 1946 to the leadership role adopted by the UK in the establishment of the International Criminal Court in 2002.

7. The United Kingdom's commitment to the United Nations is illustrated in its impressive record of membership of United Nations bodies. The United Kingdom has been a member of the Economic and Social Council (ECOSOC) and of the Commission on Sustainable Development for all of their period of operation and of the Commission on Human Rights for all but two years. In 2003 British representatives sit on the governing bodies of, amongst others, the United Nations Development Programme, the United Nations Environment Programme, the World Food Programme, the International Labour Organisation, the World Health Organisation, the United Nations Population Fund, the United Nations Children's Fund and the Office of the United Nations High Commissioner for Refugees. In addition the United Nations Department of Political Affairs, the United Nations Development Programme, and the United Nations Institute for Disarmament Research are all currently headed by Britons: Sir Kieran Prendergast, Mark Malloch Brown and Patricia Lewis. The UK pays about 5.5% of the UN Regular Budget, and makes substantial voluntary contributions to individual bodies and programmes, making a total contribution to the UN of approximately £600 million in 2002.

II INTERNATIONAL PEACE AND SECURITY

8. Article 1 of the Charter puts the maintenance of international peace and security at the heart of the Organisation's work. The Charter entrusts primary responsibility for this task to the Security Council. Occupying a unique place in the international order, the fifteen members of the Council act on behalf of the whole international community. The Council has the power to create binding obligations on all members of the UN.

9. As a permanent member of the Council, the UK therefore has a particular responsibility for international peace and security. The Government is committed to playing an active part in every aspect of the Council's work. Our contribution draws on the unique strengths and experience which come from our global diplomatic network and from our membership of the European Union, the Commonwealth, the G8, the North Atlantic Treaty Organisation and other international bodies.

10. Since the end of the Cold War, the Security Council has dealt with an increasing number of complex situations in many regions of the world. It is active over the full spectrum of dispute and crisis management. It aims to act to prevent disputes spilling into conflict, through encouraging peaceful resolution of disputes, or through specific conflict prevention measures. Where conflicts and other threats to international security are already a reality, the Council may employ more coercive measures, such as sanctions or even military intervention. In post-conflict situations, the Council can set out the framework for disarmament and reintegration of warring parties and for international peacekeeping and civilian policing operations. And in many countries emerging from conflict, the Council harnesses the efforts of the UN and the international community to help with the restoration of government structures, civil administration and the rule of law.

A united and effective Security Council

11. The fact that the Council is entrusted with its tasks by the wider UN membership means that its credibility is enhanced by acting in concert. The UK's Permanent Representative has worked with his colleagues to ensure that wherever possible consensus can be reached on an issue. A measure of our success in this aim is that all but one of the forty-one resolutions adopted by the Security Council between January and July 2003 were agreed unanimously.

12. The use, or threat, of the veto is the exception rather than the rule. The United Kingdom, for example, has not used its veto since 1989 and has not used it alone since 1972. The Government believes that the veto should be used with restraint and in accordance with the principles of the UN Charter.

13. One of the most closely followed issues on the Council's agenda is Iraq. The Council became seized of Iraq/Kuwait within hours of Saddam's invasion in 1990. It has been regularly discussed throughout the subsequent 13 years. For most of that time the Council has been united – in condemning the invasion, in imposing sanctions, in authorising the military action in 1991, in setting out the terms of the subsequent cease-fire and in directing the work of UNSCOM and later UNMOVIC. In November 2002 the Council was unanimous in adopting Security Council Resolution (SCR)1441 which gave Iraq a final chance to disarm. It was therefore all the more striking that the Council was divided earlier this year, with some permanent members threatening to use the veto, in the run up to coalition military action. But the impression this gave of a divided Council was misleading, and the overwhelming majority of the Council's work throughout that period was dealt with in a united and consensual fashion.

14. The existence of the veto, however, clearly makes it important to ensure that the five permanent members of the Council (the P5) co-operate closely on all areas of Council business. The UK has been keen to promote P5 co-ordination on a wide variety of

subjects. We have also encouraged the idea of co-operation on the ground among P5 Embassies in third countries (e.g. the Democratic Republic of Congo) where a shared analysis of the problems can help to inform joint decision making in New York.

15. Security Council resolutions are not the only means of action in the Council. The Council regularly expresses its views through statements made by the President of the Council (these are agreed by consensus among the members). And it also provides an important forum for public debate.

16. The UK has encouraged holding meetings in public more frequently, and the use of open debates at which all members of the United Nations can express their views. These debates provide a valuable opportunity for the Council to hear the concerns of other member states on subjects such as the Middle East Peace Process. The Council has also made use of imaginative measures to ensure involvement of others. The use of the Arria formula where Non-Governmental Organisations (NGOs) may address the Council has made its debates more relevant and informed.

17. The UK has also been in the lead in pioneering the use of Security Council missions, enabling the Council to become a direct actor in the countries and regions with which it deals. The first such mission in recent times, to East Timor in 1999, gained the agreement of the Indonesian government to the establishment of a UN mission and international peacekeeping force. A number of missions to Africa and other conflict-affected places have followed; some led by the UK Permanent Representative.

18. In addition, the UK Permanent Representative holds regular briefing meetings with a wide variety of groups within the UN membership. These allow an exchange of views, and ensure that the exercise of our responsibilities as a permanent member of the Council is widely understood.

19. The UK has particular responsibilities with regard to the European Union. The Treaty on the European Union obliges EU members of the Security Council to consult on their positions in the Council and keep other members of the EU informed. Arrangements to implement this obligation have been agreed between the four EU member states currently on the Security Council and include, for example, meetings at the beginning of each month to identify areas of Council business where the four countries working together can have most impact. The Council members provide regular briefings to the New York missions of the other EU countries. Where the EU has agreed common positions on subjects discussed in the Council as part of its Common Foreign and Security Policy, we promote those positions within the Council, without prejudice to our responsibilities as a permanent member of the Council.

Peaceful resolution of disputes

20. The UK is committed to working through the UN and other bodies to prevent violent conflict from emerging. Chapter VI of the UN Charter gives the Security Council a particular responsibility for putting forward proposals for the peaceful resolution of disputes. But an important role is also played by other parts of the UN system, not least the Secretary-General and his Special Representatives who can often play an important mediating role.

21. Recent developments in the Middle East Peace Process are a good example of how the various parts of the UN can work in support of one another, in combination with bilateral and multilateral diplomacy, to promote peaceful settlement of disputes. The UN Secretary-General's representative has worked together with the other members of the Quartet (the EU, US and Russia) to draw up the "Road Map" to peace. The Security Council has played a supporting role, for example adopting resolutions in 2002 explicitly endorsing the two-state solution, Security Council Resolution (SCR 1397), and calling for Israeli military withdrawal from Palestinian cities (SCR 1435) – the latter based on a text sponsored by the UK and the other European members of the Council.

22. More broadly, conflict prevention activity is becoming an increasingly important area of UN work. The UK has supported this increased emphasis, which reflects the priority given to conflict prevention work in our own foreign policy goals as demonstrated by the activities of the joint Foreign and Commonwealth Office (FCO)/Ministry of Defence (MoD)/Department for International Development (DFID) Africa and Global Conflict Prevention Pools. We warmly welcomed the thrust of the Secretary-General's Report on Conflict Prevention, published in 2001. We strongly endorse his call for the international community to move from a culture of reaction to a culture of prevention and supported the adoption of the General Assembly Resolution on the prevention of armed conflict in 2003. We also support the linkage the Secretary-General makes between conflict prevention, sustainable development and the attainment of the Millennium Development Goals. We agree that the UN will not always be the actor best placed to take the lead. But where it is, the Security Council has a particular responsibility. The UK believes it needs to engage earlier in situations which may deteriorate into armed conflict, and take appropriate preventive action.

23. The UK has also strongly supported giving increased attention to the impact of conflict on women and their participation in conflict prevention and resolution, including peace negotiations as well as raising awareness of the positive role that women can play in peace-building and reconciliation. We strongly supported the adoption of SCR 1325 in October 2000 on Women, Peace and Security and are committed to its effective implementation. This recognised the gender dimensions of conflict, and made a commitment to ensure that gender expertise is included in all UN Peacekeeping missions. In a similar vein the UK has been much involved in efforts to raise the profile of children affected by armed conflict, including through the adoption of Security Council resolutions in 2001 and 2003.

International Court of Justice (ICJ)

24. While the Security Council has a key role to play in the promotion of the peaceful settlement of disputes, the UN Charter also foresees that states should be able to submit their disputes to the International Court of Justice. The ICJ is the principal judicial organ of the UN and its Statute is an integral part of the UN Charter.

25. The Court consists of 15 members, including one judge from the UK (Judge Rosalyn Higgins DBE QC). Members of the Court are elected for periods of nine years.

26. The Court can be invited to give advisory opinions, or to settle contentious cases submitted to it by states. It also has compulsory jurisdiction where a state has declared, under Article 36 of the Statute, that it recognises the jurisdiction of the Court in legal disputes as compulsory in relation to other states accepting the same obligation.

27. The UK is alone among the permanent members of the Security Council in accepting the Court's compulsory jurisdiction. We urge others to join us and to ensure that the Court has adequate funding.

Sanctions

28. Where efforts at peaceful resolution of disputes have failed, the Security Council may decide to pursue more coercive measures. Sanctions can provide a flexible and effective means of enforcing Security Council decisions and the UK plays an important role in the formulation, implementation and enforcement of UN sanctions. The management of the sanctions regimes is carried out by UN Sanctions Committees, of which there are currently seven.

29. The UK campaigns for the more effective use of sophisticated, targeted sanctions. This policy has resulted in notable successes. There were difficult negotiations on consolidating measures aimed at tackling the threat to international peace and security posed by Al Q'aida, but these discussions culminated in the successful adoption of a series of targeted measures (asset freeze, visa restrictions, full scope arms embargo) in SCR 1390.

Angola (UNITA – Uniao Nacional para a Independencia Total de Angola) had been subject to a specific and targeted sanctions regime since 1997. The death of UNITA's leader Jonas Savimbi in February 2002 and the ensuing cease-fire in April 2002 allowed the Sanctions Committee to revisit the restrictive measures against Angola (UNITA). The sanctions against UNITA were broad: targeted travel ban, asset freeze, arms embargo, mining embargo, necessary closure of UNITA offices overseas, and embargoes on the direct or indirect import of diamonds without a valid Certificate of Origin. The sanctions measures hindered UNITA's ability to participate politically and peacefully in Angola and overseas as there was no political forum within which they could legally operate. The UK, working as co-sponsors with France, lobbied for a change in the sanctions regime. The travel ban was suspended for an initial ninety-day period. This period of suspension was extended again for a further ninety days, then lifted in November 2002. On 9 December 2002, SCR 1448 lifted all remaining measures to allow UNITA full participation in the rebuilding of Angola as a democratic society. Angola is now experiencing fragile peace.

---

30. After the conflict in Iraq earlier this year, the reconstruction of Iraq became an immediate priority. SCR 1483 co-sponsored by the UK, US and Spain lifted trade sanctions and enabled the provision of financial or economic assistance to Iraq (revenues from oil exports and the transfer of funds previously frozen under the sanctions regime will go to the Development Fund for Iraq). An arms embargo remains, as does an asset seizure on named individuals and entities. A prohibition on trade in or transfer of cultural or religious items believed to have been illegally removed from Iraq has been imposed. The resolution was wide-ranging and politically sensitive, and it is a real achievement that it was adopted in such a short timeframe. It was a demonstration of the willingness of member states to work together. The resolution was adopted with almost unanimous backing.

31. The UK is committed to appropriately targeted sanctions that are effectively implemented and enforced. We continue to work closely with partners to reform sanctions regimes, and in the future we plan to use bilateral, EU and UN fora for member states to consider UK-French proposals for a permanent international sanctions monitoring mechanism.

Military Intervention

32. In the case of more severe threats to international peace and security, the Security Council is able to authorise military intervention to remove the threat. Such intervention is relatively rare, and the suggestion of military action is frequently contentious among the UN membership, except in cases of clear aggression by one country against another, such as the invasion of South Korea in 1950 and the Iraqi invasion of Kuwait in 1990.

33. Following NATO's intervention in Kosovo, the UK proposed some guidelines for dealing with military intervention in the face of massive and systematic violations of human rights. We suggested that the development of a set of pragmatic understandings on the action to be taken in response to humanitarian crises would help the Security Council to reach consensus when such crises occur, thus ensuring effective and timely action by the international community.

34. Military intervention where it happens is often only a first step. It usually leads to a sustained international effort to keep the peace and rebuild war-torn societies.

Peacekeeping and Policing

35. The UK first participated in a UN peacekeeping force in March 1964. The mission was the United Nations Peacekeeping Force in Cyprus (UNFICYP), now in its fortieth year. Contributors throughout, the UK currently provides 415 military personnel to UNFICYP and we are considering the deployment of UK civilian police to the mission.

36. Since 1964, UK troops, military observers and civilian police have served in eighteen UN missions, in Africa, the Balkans, the Middle East and South East Asia. Most early peacekeeping operations were in response to inter-state conflict. In recent years, however, peace keeping has more often addressed intra-state conflicts where governments have been unable or unwilling to carry out their normal peace-time functions. As well as carrying out the "classic" or "traditional" peacekeeping tasks of cease-fire monitoring and provision of buffer zones between opposing parties, UK personnel have been called upon to undertake the full range of "complex" peacekeeping tasks. These include the negotiation and implementation of peace agreements, the promotion of respect for human rights, the organisation and monitoring of elections, disarmament, demobilisation and reintegration, and reform and capacity building of military, police and other civilian institutions.

Current UK Personnel Contribution to UN Missions	
UK military in UN Missions:	
Sierra Leone (UNAMSIL) DRC (MONUC) Ethiopia/Eritrea (UNMEE) Cyprus (UNFICYP) Georgia (UNOMIG)	22 (7 HQ staff including Chief of Staff) 6 (all HQ staff including Chief of Staff) 4 (all HQ staff including Force Comdr.) 415 (12 UNHQ; 23 UK HQ) 7 (1 in Sector HQ)
Total	**454**
UK civilian police in UN missions:	
Timor-Leste (UNMISET) Sierra Leone (UNAMSIL) Kosovo (UNMIK)	11 10 133
Total	**154**

37. In addition, the UK has 1,267 personnel serving in Bosnia, 304 in Kosovo and 415 in Afghanistan, all UN authorised missions. There are also three senior UK military officers serving in the Department of Peacekeeping Operations (DPKO) in New York.

38. It is our responsibility as a permanent member of the Security Council to support the UN in its efforts to maintain international peace and security. It is also in our national interest to prevent and resolve conflict. Conflict spreads and can quickly become "our problem" as well as "their problem". Resources are limited and over-stretched. We therefore try to ensure that we target our resources on where we can best add value and make a difference to the effectiveness of UN peacekeeping.

39. We have done this in a number of different ways. In the Security Council we have fought for clear, robust and realistic mandates for peacekeeping missions. In the Fifth Committee, the UK has worked to ensure that there is stricter budgetary control and financial management of peacekeeping operations and that missions are cost effective. In DPKO in New York and in the field we have offered highly qualified candidates to fill key positions, on the basis that the best contribution we can make, given limited resources, is to share expertise and best practice.

40. The UK is currently the fifth largest contributor to the UN peacekeeping budget. Our share of the assessed budget is roughly 6.9%, although this is likely to rise to around 7.4% in financial year 2003/4. Our forecast expenditure on UN peacekeeping, assessed and non-assessed contributions, in this financial year, is around £191 million. This expenditure is met from the peacekeeping element of the joint FCO/DFID/MOD Conflict Prevention Pools, which also meet the costs of non-UN peacekeeping (NATO, OSCE, and EU) and conflict prevention and peace-building programme activity. The total expenditure on peacekeeping in this financial year under the Conflict Prevention Pools (Africa and Global) is forecast at £380 million.

41. Given our high financial stake in UN peacekeeping and our determination that UN peace operations should be more effective, the UK is firmly committed to pushing forward the peacekeeping reform process, initiated by the Brahimi Report on UN Peace

Operations of August 2000. With the endorsement of the Prime Minister, we fully supported the package of recommendations in the report, in particular: the strengthening of mandates; improved co-operation and co-ordination between UN agencies and departments; the creation of an early warning information system; the establishment of strategic deployment stocks at the UN logistics base in Brindisi and the strengthening of DPKO in New York. With the exception of the early warning system, which was opposed by some members of the Non-Aligned Movement (NAM), out of misplaced concern that it could involve intelligence gathering, many of the recommendations in the Brahimi Report have been implemented.

42. The UK, along with other like-minded member states and UN DPKO, recognises that, although much was achieved by the Brahimi Report, much more remains to be done to improve UN peacekeeping. Improvements in New York need to be translated into improved operational effectiveness in the field.

43. In the Special Committee on Peacekeeping (C34) in March 2003 and in other international fora, the UK has been promoting seven key priorities for UN peace operations:

- Pre-deployment training (in particular for senior mission personnel);

- Best practices and the application of lessons learned;

- Rapid deployment and logistics;

- Code of conduct;

- Civilian policing;

- Human resources reform;

- Co-operation with regional organisations, e.g. ECOWAS, to address conflict.

44. These priorities tie in with those outlined by the Under-Secretary General for Peacekeeping, Jean-Marie Guehenno, in his address to the Fourth Committee in October 2002.

45. In the last two years we have worked closely with DPKO, and with Mr Guehenno in particular, on how best the UK might assist in enhancing the UN's peacekeeping and peace-building capacity. In June 2003 Mr Guehenno visited the UK. In addition to participating in round table discussions on African peacekeeping and thematic peacekeeping reform issues, Mr Guehenno took part in the UN Reform Seminar hosted by Bill Rammell on 19 June 2003. He also gave a speech at Chatham House on the future challenges of UN peacekeeping and visited the Permanent Joint Headquarters (PJHQ) in Northwood, for a demonstration on UK military planning and to see whether UN peace operations might benefit from a similar standing HQ arrangement.

46. The UK's input to the peacekeeping reform process is backed by the Conflict Prevention Pools. The UN "Brahimi" Programme Strategy under the Global Conflict Prevention Pool (GCPP) funds activities to strengthen the capacity of the UN to plan, manage and undertake peacekeeping and peace-building operations. Projects developed by the UN Strategy have included international "train the trainer" courses for civilian police officers. Run by Centrex (formerly the Bramshill Police Staff College) in Accra, Gaborone, Buenos Aires, Beijing, Amman, Budapest and Warsaw, the courses have been attended by more than thirty existing or potential personnel contributors to UN peace operations.

47. The UN GCPP Strategy has also funded a series of civil/military peacekeeping exercises in Buenos Aires, Bangkok and Dakar, with plans for a further exercise in Bangladesh within this financial year. A number of seminars on, e.g. the Protection of Civilians in Armed Conflict and the Brahimi Report have been funded by the Strategy, as have UK/India and UK/Pakistan peacekeeping bilaterals. A UK peacekeeping website (www.peacekeeping.co.uk) is being developed using GCPP funds and there are plans for an Open University module on peacekeeping based on the peacekeeping exercises. Under the Strategy the UK has also funded the preparation of a UN handbook on multi-dimensional operations and projects, designed to raise awareness of issues affecting women when UN operations are deployed. The GCPP Strategy will support the development of a virtual resource centre from which those at HQ and field level can draw information to ensure that gender is mainstreamed into peace operations. MOD experts have worked with DPKO to design a logistics project for an improved warehouse management system at the UN logistics base in Brindisi. Mr Guehenno commended the UK for this assistance in his statement prior to the C34 in March this year.

48. A major initiative under the UN Strategy has been the commissioning of four comprehensive studies on the UN peace operations in Sierra Leone, East Timor, Afghanistan and Kosovo ("A Review of Peace Operations: A case for change", http://ipi.sspp.kcl.ac.uk/peaceoperationsreview). Undertaken by King's College London (KCL) these studies have proved to be a valuable tool in terms of identifying next steps for improving UN peace operations. UN DPKO has agreed to engage with UK officials to discuss implementation of the recommendations. And DPKO has invited the UK to contribute to a workshop which the Training and Evaluation Service (TES) is organising in South America in the near future.

> ### UK's role in restoring peace, security and stability in Sierra Leone
>
> Sierra Leone is regarded as a UN success story. UK support and commitment to restoring peace, security and stability in Sierra Leone has been critical to that success. The UK has pursued a strategy to draw the rebels into the peace process, to reintegrate former combatants and to rebuild the country. The intervention of UK forces in May 2000 to assist the Government of Sierra Leone (GOSL) and the floundering UN peacekeeping mission in Sierra Leone (UNAMSIL) was a turning point in the peace process. Our Over the Horizon military deployments have boosted the confidence of the GOSL and UNAMSIL. This was a demonstration of what a joined up, multi-dimensional approach to conflict resolution can achieve.
>
> More than 50,000 fighters from the rebel and other militias have disarmed throughout the country. More than 1,000 child soldiers have been released. Peaceful and credible elections in May 2002 saw President Kabbah of the Sierra Leone's People's Party (SLPP) re-elected. UNAMSIL began to draw down in November 2002.
>
> However the peace is still fragile and more needs to be done to secure a peaceful future for Sierra Leone, with the GOSL assuming responsibility for the maintenance of law and order throughout the country and on its borders. Post-conflict the UK has continued to assist the GOSL to establish more effective and accountable armed forces and police, both bilaterally and as part of UNAMSIL. More than 10,000 Sierra Leonean soldiers have received basic training from the UK-led International Military and Advisory Training Team (IMATT). Ten UK police officers have recently joined the Civilian Police (CivPol) component of UNAMSIL in providing training, monitoring and mentoring to the Sierra Leone Police (SLP).

Post-conflict assistance

49. Peacekeeping is just one part of the UN's contribution to rebuilding societies recovering from conflict. Much of the wider work is undertaken by the Funds, Programmes and Specialised Agencies, which are described later in this paper (Section III). The UN's involvement can vary from a relatively small scale peace-building mission, such as that in Guinea-Bissau (headed by a British UN official), to the considerable assistance mission in Afghanistan, or the full-scale Transitional Administration which oversaw East Timor's move to independence.

50. Where the Security Council establishes UN assistance missions, the UK plays a key role in helping to determine their mandate. The extent of UN involvement is tailored in each case to the needs of the particular situation. In many instances, the UK is heavily engaged in providing political, financial and human resources support to the UN missions.

International Criminal Tribunals

51. An important aspect of many post-conflict situations and in conflict prevention measures is the need to deal with past crimes. As a strong proponent of international justice, the UK has been actively engaged in the major bodies set up over the last decade

to try individuals accused of genocide, war crimes and crimes against humanity. Our over-arching aim is to see enshrined the principle of individual criminal responsibility for such crimes. At the same time, to enjoy a wide base of public support, international justice must be delivered efficiently and effectively, and the UK uses its influence as a major budget contributor and a UN Security Council member to work for this.

52. Civil wars in the 1990s resulted in unimaginable suffering for millions of innocent people amidst violent conflicts during which every conceivable violation of human rights and international law was perpetrated up to and including genocide. Because of the lack of a permanent international court to try individuals responsible for these tragic events, two ad hoc International Criminal Tribunals were set up by the UN Security Council to try those involved in the conflicts in the former Yugoslavia and Rwanda (respectively ICTY and ICTR). The International Criminal Court (ICC), which was established in July 2002, was set up to try individuals responsible for the most serious international crimes: war crimes, crimes against humanity and genocide. So far 139 states have signed and 91 have ratified the ICC statutes.

International Criminal Tribunal for Yugoslavia (ICTY)

53. The ICTY was established in 1993 by the Security Council in response to the serious violations of international humanitarian law committed in the territory of the former Yugoslavia since 1991, and as a response to the threat to international peace and security those violations posed.

54. ICTY (and ICTR, see below) is funded by assessed contributions levied on UN member states. The UK contributes $7.85 million (around £5 million) to the current US$128.5 million budget. British citizens are engaged at all levels of work in the tribunal. The most prominent is Judge Richard May, Presiding Judge in the Milosevic case; Geoffrey Nice QC is leading for the Prosecution.

International Criminal Tribunal for Rwanda (ICTR)

55. The International Criminal Tribunal for Rwanda (ICTR) was established by the Security Council in 1994. The ICTR was established for the prosecution of persons responsible for genocide and other serious violations of international humanitarian law committed in the territory of Rwanda between 1 January 1994 and 31 December 1994. It may also deal with the prosecution of Rwandan citizens responsible for genocide and other such violations of international law committed in the territory of neighbouring states during the same period.

56. The ICTR costs around $106 million per year. The UK contribution for the calendar year 2003 is around $5.8 million (approximately £4.1 million).

57. There are concerns, some of which are shared by the British Government, about the expense of the Tribunals (each has cost around $700 million to date), the time taken to prosecute cases and the relatively low number of prosecutions at the ICTR. There is also some concern that the geographical distance from the area where the crimes took place makes this a remote and unsatisfactory form of justice for the victims. We are working for improvements but other factors need to be balanced. The Tribunals are dealing with cases of great complexity and broad scope. They have generated important, and in some cases, ground breaking case law. The trial of former President Milosevic at ICTY is the first time that a former Head of State is being tried for genocide. At ICTR, Jean

Kambanda became the first former Head of Government to be convicted of genocide. The landmark ICTR judgment in the Akayesu case broke new ground in defining rape in international law and by holding that rape could constitute genocide. On 28 August, the Security Council adopted SCR 1503 which splits the post of Chief Prosecutor for the Tribunals: a proposal which the UK supports, since the Tribunals can be expected to function more effectively if they each have a dedicated Prosecutor.

58. More recently, the UN has experimented with 'mixed' courts i.e. bodies consisting of both domestic and international judges and staff:

Special Court for Sierra Leone (SCSL)

59. The Special Court for Sierra Leone (SCSL) was set up under an agreement between the Government of Sierra Leone and the UN signed in January 2002. Its mandate is to prosecute "persons who bear the greatest responsibility for serious violations" of international humanitarian law and domestic law committed in Sierra Leone since 30 November 1996. The first permanent officials of the Court arrived in Freetown in July 2002.

60. The UK has been heavily involved in the Court so far. A British national, Robin Vincent, is Registrar of the Court. We sit on the Management Committee, which assists the Court by providing advice and policy direction on all non-judicial aspects of its operations, including questions of efficiency, approving its budget and encouraging other states to co-operate with and contribute to the Court.

61. The Court relies on voluntary contributions. The UK has committed £6.6 million (out of an overall budget of around £40 million) over the three-year life span of the Court. This is a percentage contribution of 16.5%. Funding is a source of concern: the Court currently faces a shortfall of around £14 million. We have undertaken an active lobbying campaign, involving the Foreign Secretary, in support of the UN Secretary-General's call earlier this year for additional funds.

Khmer Rouge Tribunal

62. In June 2003, after many years of negotiation, the UN and the Government of Cambodia signed an agreement establishing "Extraordinary Chambers" of the Cambodia Court – to try senior Khmer Rouge figures accused of genocide, war crimes and crimes against humanity between April 1975 and January 1979 when almost one million people (20% of the population) lost their lives. The Cambodian National Assembly is expected to ratify the Agreement this autumn. Despite international concerns as to whether the provisions in the Agreement relating to the structure and organisation of the Chambers would fully ensure their credibility, it is hoped that with the good will of all sides, these operating issues can be resolved quickly and the Tribunal can be established soon. The number of trials has not been determined, but could be as many as ten to twelve. The Chambers will consist of a mixture of international and domestic judges.

63. The cost of the international component is currently estimated at US$ 18.5 million and will be funded via voluntary contributions. The UK will be making a contribution once the budgetary requirements are clarified.

New threats – New responses

64. While the Security Council's work remains dominated by conventional armed conflicts between and within states, its attention has become increasingly focussed on new challenges to international peace and security. Following the events of 11th September 2001, the response to international terrorism has been an urgent priority. Proliferation issues too have risen close to the top of the agenda.

65. The Counter Terrorism Committee (CTC) was established following the events of 11th September by SCR 1373 under Chapter VII of the UN Charter. SCR 1373 went beyond the scope of existing international treaties on terrorism, imposing uniform obligations on all states to suppress and prevent financial and other support for terrorism. The Counter-Terrorism Committee (CTC) – which is a sub-committee of the Security Council, with the same membership – monitors implementation of the resolution. States are required to report regularly to the CTC on domestic measures taken to combat terrorism.

66. The UK has played a central role in the CTC since its establishment and for the first 18 months until April 2003 Sir Jeremy Greenstock, UK Permanent Representative to the UN, chaired the Committee.

67. Initial priorities were to encourage all states to put in place legislation covering all aspects of SCR 1373 (including becoming party to the twelve existing international conventions and protocols relating to terrorism) and preventing and suppressing the financing of terrorism. Future stages of the Committee's work will consider states' executive machinery (e.g. police, customs, immigration) covering all aspects of SCR 1373 and controls preventing the access to weapons (including those of mass destruction) by terrorists.

68. The response received has been positive with all 191 member states of the UN having submitted at least one report and 148 two or more. The Committee has started to review third-round reports. In July 2001, the UK was only one of two countries to have ratified all 12 existing counter-terrorism conventions. Since then, that figure has risen to 37 with a further 38 having ratified 10 or 11. The CTC has also established a dialogue with relevant international and regional organisations to encourage greater co-operation in the international effort to combat terrorism.

69. Even though no longer in the Chair, the UK continues to be a major contributor to the work of the CTC and is determined to ensure that it maintains a continued high political profile for counter-terrorism work. As the number of countries engaging with the CTC has grown so has its workload and it is imperative that the CTC should have the tools to do the job.

70. The Security Council has yet to tackle proliferation questions in as concerted a way as it has focussed on terrorism. However, it has devoted attention to individual elements of this agenda, and has taken action with regard to certain countries of concern. The UK has encouraged the Council to act to counter the threats of proliferation from both conventional arms and weapons of mass destruction. In addition, proliferation issues are dealt with by other parts of the UN system, in particular bodies such as the International Atomic Energy Agency and the Organisation for the Prohibition of Chemical Weapons which oversee obligations under the relevant non-proliferation treaties. The General

Assembly and Department of Disarmament Affairs also deal with small arms and light weapons (SALW) issues. The growing international concern over the proliferation of Man Portable Air Defence Systems (MANPADS) highlighted at the G8 Summit has led to the UN also beginning to deal with the issue. It was de facto agreed in July that UN members should report MANPADS transfers as part of their UN Register of Conventional Arms submissions.

71. In relation to conventional arms, the UK has been leading the implementation of various aspects of the UN Programme of Action (PoA) on SALW. The UK has given the United Nations Development Programme £7.5 million over three years for a global programme of weapons collection, stockpile management, capacity building and destruction within the context of disarmament, demobilisation, reintegration and community development. At the Biennial Meeting of states to review the Programme held in July 2003 the UK chaired a meeting of interested states to discuss an ongoing initiative on strengthening export controls to tackle the spread of SALW. The UK also spoke on mobilising resources to combat small arms and hosted a meeting on donor co-ordination where DFID launched their booklet "Tackling Poverty by Reducing Armed Violence". The Security Council too has been active on SALW in a regional context, adopting, for example, a Presidential Statement in March 2003 on the problem of small arms proliferation in West Africa as a factor fuelling conflict in that region.

72. Tackling the proliferation of Weapons of Mass Destruction (WMD) is one of the UK's highest foreign policy priorities, and we would like to see the UN playing a more consistent and active role in this area. The history of ten years of Security Council resolutions, sanctions, inspections, and finally military action to deal with Iraq's prohibited weapons programmes has been well documented elsewhere. Whatever the differences of view within the Security Council on the military action that was taken, there was no disagreement at earlier stages about the threat posed by WMD programmes. We wish to encourage a more united approach to proliferators elsewhere in the world, and greater agreement on the best way of tackling threats from WMD.

III ECONOMIC AND SOCIAL DEVELOPMENT

General Assembly

73. The General Assembly is the main deliberative organ of the United Nations. It is composed of representatives of all 191 member states, each of which has one vote. The work of the United Nations derives largely from the decisions of the General Assembly.

74. The General Assembly's regular session is held from September to December each year. All discussion on economic and social issues take place in the Second (Economic and Financial Committee) and Third Committees (Social, Humanitarian and Cultural Committee).

Economic and Social Council (ECOSOC)

75. Over 70% of the human and financial resources of the UN are devoted to sustainable development, including economic and social development. The Economic and Social Council (ECOSOC) is the principal body that co-ordinates the economic and social work of the United Nations. ECOSOC reports to the UN General Assembly.

76. ECOSOC co-ordinates the work of the Functional Commissions, Funds, Programmes, and Specialised Agencies of the UN. It is mandated to provide policy guidance to these bodies and review the operational activities of the various bodies. It also co-ordinates the humanitarian work of the UN.

77. In practice, ECOSOC consists of 54 member states (the UK is currently a member) which meet at a four-week substantive session each July, alternating between New York and Geneva. The session includes a high-level segment, at which national cabinet ministers and chiefs of international agencies focus their attention on a selected theme of global significance. In 2003 the high-level segment covered "Promoting an integrated approach to rural development in developing countries for poverty eradication and sustainable development" and was attended by DFID Minister Hilary Benn.

78. In addition to the substantive sessions, ECOSOC meets each April with finance ministers heading key committees of the Bretton Woods institutions – the World Bank and the International Monetary Fund – to focus on areas where co-operation and policy guidance is necessary. The UK encourages greater co-operation between the UN, the International Financial Institutions and the World Trade Organisation (WTO).

79. The UK is an active participant in ECOSOC, and would like to see the body providing more effective co-ordination and policy advice. The UK recently took part in a UN Working Group that looked at how ECOSOC might be reformed. Some of the key recommendations from this group, such as revamping ECOSOC sessions to focus them on particular themes from UN Conferences, will soon be implemented.

Sustainable Development – Development and poverty reduction

United Nations Development Programme (UNDP)

80. The UN Development Programme is the central UN vehicle for co-ordination of the UN system in individual countries, through the UN Development Assistance Framework process (UNDAF). It also manages and finances provision of the UN Resident Co-ordinator posts that UNDP operates in 166 countries, working with these countries on their own solutions to development challenges, and providing policy and technical advice and other assistance for development.

81. At the Millennium Summit held in September 2000, 187 member states pledged to achieve the Millennium Development Goals (MDGs), including the overarching goal of cutting poverty in half by 2015. All the UN agencies are working within their mandates towards achieving the MDGs. UNDP has the role of advocate and scorekeeper of progress towards the achievement of the MDGs. UNDP also has a key role in helping achieve the related goals, on issues such as access to sanitation and energy, agreed at the September 2002 World Summit on Sustainable Development (WSSD).

82. DFID is the largest of nine donors to UNDP's Millennium Programme, contributing £3.5 million over three years. The programme supports the setting of strategies to achieve each of the MDGs, the monitoring and reporting of progress at both national and global level, and national and global campaigning in their support.

83. To focus more closely on its strengths, UNDP has concentrated its activities in six areas: democratic governance, poverty reduction, crisis prevention and recovery, energy/environment, Information Communications Technology and HIV/AIDS.

84. The UNDP Executive Board includes representatives from 36 nations, on a rotating basis, of which the UK is currently one. The UK is the sixth largest donor to UNDP's regular resources and the fifth largest overall in 2002 with a total contribution of $135 million (£90 million). This accounted for 7.3% of UNDP's total receipts of $1,848 million.

85. DFID has set out the objectives for its partnership with UNDP in an Institutional Strategy Paper (ISP). The ISP has ten specific objectives, which outline the areas of UK support. DFID currently supports Technical Co-operation projects worth £2.1 million. The objectives include:

- Strengthening leadership of the Millennium Development Goals (which contributes to UNDP's larger MDG programme);

- Partnerships with NGOs, Civil Society and the private sector;

- Improving programme effectiveness;

- Staff development programme for Deputy Resident Representatives.

86. The UK is supporting UNDP's programme of organisational reforms. Among these is a new externally managed, meritocratic, competence based assessment centre process for Resident Co-ordinator posts.

87. Since 2000, the UK has also supported UNDP's capacity to provide an effective response to conflicts and natural disasters, through a package of assistance to the Bureau for Crisis Prevention and Recovery (BCPR). DFID is entering the third phase of support to BCPR (with an overall value of £5.8 million).

United Nations Children's Fund (UNICEF)

88. The UN Children's Fund's mandate is 'to advocate for the protection of children's rights, to help meet their basic needs and to expand their opportunities to reach their full potential'. UNICEF is guided by the Convention on the Rights of the Child, which recognises children's special needs as inalienable rights and guarantees those rights under law.

89. UNICEF works in 158 countries. UNICEF is governed by a 36 member Executive Board, of which the UK is a member. Unlike any other UN agency, it has two funding sources: Government 65% and Non-Government 35%. UNICEF receipts for 2002 were £589 million of which the UK provided £17 million in core resources and £27 million in other resources, making the UK the fourth largest donor.

90. An Institutional Strategy Paper (ISP) underpins the UK's collaboration with UNICEF. Key among the objectives are to:

- Support UNICEF where it is well placed to contribute to the achievement of the Millennium Development Goals (MDGs) (including the rights of children to health, education, protection and equality);

- Strengthen UNICEF so that it can make a more effective contribution to the international development effort;

- Strengthen UNICEF's capacity to respond more effectively to humanitarian crises, to meet the needs of children in armed conflict situations, and to take forward its mines awareness programme.

91. In order to support UK objectives, DFID is currently working to strengthen UNICEF's institutional capacity in policy debates on poverty reduction strategies and sector-wide plans at country, regional and global level, as well as to accelerate mine awareness programming and advocacy and promote universal ratification and implementation of the Ottawa Convention. The UK is also encouraging UNICEF to better integrate humanitarian and development programming more fully.

92. DFID and UNICEF work together in many developing countries. For example, the UK is currently working in partnership with UNICEF and the Government of Bangladesh to reduce the mortality and morbidity caused by diarrhoea and other water borne diseases by improving rural hygiene, sanitation and water supply.

Food and Agriculture Organisation (FAO)

93. The Food and Agricultural Organisation (FAO) is the lead agency for food and agriculture, including forestry and fisheries, within the UN system. It is a Specialised Agency, governed by its 190 members and associates through a biennial Conference, supported by a 49-member Council, which draws in its turn on specialised sub-committees dealing with such issues as finance, programmes, agriculture, fisheries, forestry and food security.

94. The Organisation's mandate is to collect and disseminate information on food, agriculture and nutrition; to act as a forum for discussion and negotiation and to set commonly agreed standards. The mandate also extends to provision of technical assistance to Governments.

95. Based in Rome, FAO is one of the largest UN Specialised Agencies. FAO's total annual turnover is projected at some $645 million in the 2002-03 biennium. The UK is the fifth largest subscriber (£10.9 million in 2003) with a programme of some £6.5 million annually over the next few years.

96. FAO matters to developing countries because of the core importance of agricultural productivity to poverty alleviation and economic growth, and because of their interests in food insecurity; global and regional commons issues; access to high-income export markets; the competitive advantage of their agri-food industries (strongly influenced by food standards); protection of rights to genetic resources; information for decision-making; and various kinds of technical assistance. The FAO is important to developed countries because of their interests in food safety and food standards; bio-safety for plants and animals, global and regional commons issues and statistical information.

97. DFID is the lead UK Department for FAO, with support from the Department for Environment, Food and Rural Affairs (DEFRA), the Food Standards Agency, the Forestry Commission and FCO. The UK influences the FAO and its membership through active participation in the Council and its sub-committees, and through extra-budgetary funding we provide for institutional strengthening. UK strategic priorities are to:

- Ensure that the FAO makes an appropriate and effective contribution to the Millennium Development Goals relating to poverty, hunger and environmental sustainability;

- Strengthen FAO's relevance and its niche in the global architecture by clarifying and promoting its role as a source of international public goods;

- Encourage FAO to play a full part in the UN reform agenda and to strengthen its partnerships with other agencies;

- Improve the governance of the FAO by reintroducing term limits for the Director-General's post at the November 2003 General Conference;

- Support management reforms, with particular emphasis on staff, who are FAO's chief asset, and the progressive overhaul of systems for planning, budgeting, reporting and evaluation, based on the principle of results-based management.

United Nations Educational, Scientific and Cultural Organisation (UNESCO)

98. DFID is the lead UK Department for UNESCO, since the UK's primary interest in the organisation is its potential to contribute to the achievement of the Millennium Development Goals. Other Government Departments including Department for Culture Media and Sport, Department for Education and Skills, Department of Health, Department for Trade and Industry (DTI) and the FCO also have an interest. The UK's current share of UNESCO's assessed contributions is £12.4 million.

99. UK priorities are to see UNESCO:

- Give precedence to achieving the Millennium Development Goals for education;

- Work to improve the production of policy-relevant and internationally comparable statistics on education in developing countries and countries in transition;

- Ensure that all programmes incorporate systems for monitoring and show clear evidence of impact and assessment of outcomes;

- Participate more fully in the wider UN reform agenda and build effective partnerships with other agencies.

100. The UK influences UNESCO, a Specialised Agency, through the governing bodies of which we are a member, but also increasingly through our active role in the EU Group, the Geneva Group of key donors, and ad hoc working groups.

101. The UK has been a member of the Executive Board since we rejoined UNESCO in 1997 after an absence of twelve years. Since 1997, with a new senior management team at UNESCO, we have succeeded in incorporating some of the UK's priorities (e.g. eradication of poverty, Education for All, access for all to information and communication technologies) into UNESCO's medium term strategy. There is much more to be done, however, in terms of focussing UNESCO's activities more specifically on the achievement of the Millennium Development Goals.

United Nations Population Fund (UNFPA)

102. The UN Population Fund (UNFPA) was set up to promote population activities within the UN, including strengthening capacity in family planning and reproductive health, helping developing countries formulate population policies suited to their sustainable development needs and raising awareness globally about demographic trends and challenges.

103. The UN Population Fund is the largest UN provider of sexual reproductive health assistance to developing countries, championing and supporting action to enable women to choose in matters of reproduction, to go through pregnancy more safely, and to prevent HIV/AIDS. The Fund also plays a key role in assisting countries, including by strengthening capacity in relation to population censuses and surveys and health data collection systems. The UK has a strong interest in UNFPA reproductive health activities, especially those tackling the global HIV/AIDS crisis. UNFPA is one of seven UN agencies that co-sponsor the UN Joint Programme on HIV/AIDS.

104. The UK's contributions to UNFPA's core budget are voluntary and are currently £18 million per annum. The total UK contribution amounts to about 9.4% of UNFPA's 2002 budget of about US$350 million. The UK's relationship with UNFPA is covered by an Institutional Strategy Paper (ISP) "Working in Partnership with UNFPA" which was developed in close consultation with UNFPA and a range of stakeholders. Our overall objective in working with UNFPA is that it should play an effective role in supporting reproductive health and rights at country level within the context of national poverty reduction strategies.

105. In 1994, UNFPA was Secretariat to the landmark International Conference on Population and Development, which put the right to reproductive health at the centre of population and development issues. This conference agreed International Development Targets (IDTs), which then became Millennium Development Goals (MDGs), for reducing maternal and child mortality and for attaining universal access to reproductive health by 2015. UNFPA has been an effective and outspoken champion for reproductive health and rights, but has been the victim of attacks and unsubstantiated allegations from religious conservative groups who take a different view on these issues.

Commission for Social Development (CSocD)

106. A number of Government departments, including the FCO and Department for Work and Pensions (DWP), have an interest in the Commission for Social Development (CSocD), particularly its work on employment, social security and international labour standards. The UK Government's priority for CSocD is to promote employment in the context of integrated social and economic policies. In doing so, we encourage the adoption of effective national employment policies as key to development and combating poverty.

107. In promoting the issue of employment at CSocD, we have sought to highlight the importance of the internationally agreed core labour standards and the 1998 International Labour Organisation (ILO) Declaration of Fundamental Principles and Rights at Work which is based on those standards. They cover freedom of association and the right to collective bargaining, the elimination of forced and child labour and the ending of discrimination in employment.

20

108. The UK has also taken an active role in CSocD discussions on a number of issues that have subsequently taken on greater international significance, such as the follow-up to the World Summit on Social Development. More recently we participated fully and actively in discussions on the issues of older persons, which led to the Madrid International Plan and the Berlin Regional Plan on Ageing.

United Nations Development Fund for Women (UNIFEM)

109. The mandate of the UN Development Fund for Women (UNIFEM) is to support innovative activities in UN development work benefiting women and to serve as a catalyst to ensure the involvement of women in mainstream development activities. Its current work programme focuses on strengthening women's economic capacities and rights; bringing a gender perspective into governance and leadership; and promoting women's human rights and the elimination of violence. It reports to the UNDP Executive Board.

110. The UK is currently UNIFEM's largest donor, contributing £3 million a year in core funding. UK objectives in supporting UNIFEM are to help it:

- Consolidate and build its strategic role in building gender mainstreaming capacity in UN, in the context of reform;

- Continue streamlining its portfolio to focus on key areas of innovation, suitable for mainstream implementation;

- To introduce new impact assessment and lesson learning systems.

111. A recent DFID review of UNIFEM performance showed it was making good progress in all of these areas, but needed to further strengthen its strategic engagement at the field level. UNIFEM has enthusiastically embraced the UN reform agenda, and is making rapid progress in key areas such as results-based management.

112. A new institutional partnership is to be developed with UNIFEM by the end of 2004. This is expected to focus on supporting UNIFEM in strengthening its strategic contribution to the achievement of the Millennium Development Goals and helping it build its operational and strategic partnerships. The partnership will also focus on helping it improve its effectiveness by strengthening its results-based management framework and associated lesson learning and knowledge sharing systems and the adoption of a rights based approach to programming.

113. UNIFEM is currently enjoying a high profile in UN due to its work on women, peace and security, and involvement in the groundbreaking SCR 1325. UNIFEM recently completed a major study of the impact of conflict on women (with UK funding) as Volume 1 of "Progress of the World's Women" as a follow up to this resolution.

Commission on the Status of Women (CSW)

114. The Commission on the Status of Women was established as a Functional Commission of the Economic and Social Council to prepare recommendations on promoting women's rights in political, economic, civil, social and educational fields. Following the 1995 Fourth World Conference on Women ('Beijing Conference'), the UN General Assembly (UNGA) mandated CSW to oversee follow-up to the Beijing Platform for Action.

115. The UK, led by the Women and Equality Unit (WEU) of the Department of Trade and Industry, actively participates and contributes (through the EU) to the annual session of the CSW. Voluntary UK funding is provided to support the work of the UN Secretariat to prepare for the annual session.

116. At the 2003 session, CSW considered two main themes:

- Participation and access of women to the media and information and communication technology;

- Women's human rights and elimination of all forms of violence against women and girls.

117. CSW membership facilitates the UK's efforts to promote the advancement of women and gender equality within the international community, as well as ensuring that UK experience and interests are taken into account in shaping the international gender equality agenda. The UK's priorities for the body include co-ordinating the implementation and monitoring of the Beijing Platform for Action and the outcome document of the UN General Assembly's 23rd Special Session on "Women, Peace and Development".

118. The UK has been at the forefront of work on gender mainstreaming within the UN system. In 2003, the UK ran a resolution at CSW on 'mainstreaming a gender perspective into all policies and programmes in the UN system'. The UK resolution offers specific direction to CSW and the Economic and Social Council (ECOSOC) on an effective gender mainstreaming strategy across the UN system.

UN Conference on Trade and Development (UNCTAD)

119. The United Nations Conference on Trade and Development (UNCTAD) is the principal organ of the UN General Assembly in the area of trade and development. UNCTAD discharges its mandate via a mix of policy analysis, arranging consensus building (primarily through inter-Governmental meetings) and technical assistance.

120. Despite its name, UNCTAD is a standing body and meets in Ministerial session once every four years (on average). The last Ministerial, UNCTAD X, which took place in Bangkok in February 2000, was widely considered to be a success. UNCTAD XI will take place in June 2004 in Sao Paolo.

121. Both the DTI and DFID take an interest in UNCTAD. External donors, including the UK, fund many of the technical assistance projects undertaken by UNCTAD. Since 1998, the UK has committed over £10 million to fund (or part-fund) ten separate projects with UNCTAD, including work on preparing developing countries for globalisation, helping developing countries accede to the WTO and building developing countries' capacity in the areas of competition policy, services and trade and the environment.

122. UK priorities for UNCTAD focus on what UNCTAD can do to enable developing countries to benefit from international trade, both through the provision of analysis of international trade policy issues and through the provision of trade-related technical assistance and capacity building.

123. The Governing Body of UNCTAD is the Trade and Development Board, which comprises the membership of the organisation. The UK plays a full role in discussions in the Trade and Development Board and, during the recent Mid Term Review of UNCTAD X, the UK chaired a stock-taking exercise on the implementation of the commitments and work programme agreed to in the Bangkok Plan of Action agreed at UNCTAD X.

International Fund for Agricultural Development (IFAD)

124. The International Fund for Agricultural Development (IFAD) finances agricultural development projects, primarily for food production, in developing countries. It is a Specialised Agency of the UN, based in Rome. A Governing Council appoints an 18-member Executive Board. Membership of the Fund is a unique partnership between OECD, OPEC and developing countries.

125. IFAD's mission is to enable the rural poor to combat poverty and hunger. Its core business is making loans to national governments for projects focussed on micro-level solutions. IFAD reaches 34 million rural households (169 million people). Women make up 40% of the target group.

126. The Fund's operations are financed by replenishment, investment income and loan reflows. In the recently completed Sixth Replenishment the UK pledged $30 million (around 7 per cent of the OECD share) out of a total of some $520 million, plus $10 million towards a new multi-donor innovation fund. Annual commitments by the Fund are currently some $450 million ($420 million as loans; $30 million as technical assistance grants). More than 80% of lending is on highly concessional terms, with Africa as the principal beneficiary. IFAD has a comparatively small project portfolio and its loans typically range from $4-12 million. Most involve co-financing with other donors.

127. DFID is the lead UK Department for IFAD. The UK influences the Fund and its membership through active participation in the Governing Council and Executive Board and in ad hoc working groups and committees. UK strategic priorities are to:

- Encourage the introduction of a Performance-Based Allocation System for IFAD's lending programme;

- Sharpen and reinforce IFAD's role as an innovator in relation to rural poverty and its capacity to learn lessons and share these with partners who can replicate and scale up successful new approaches;

- Help IFAD and the membership devise cost-effective ways of enlarging the Fund's involvement in country-driven policy discussion and implementation.

- Work to ensure that the forthcoming Independent External Evaluation of IFAD is both comprehensive and authoritative.

Statistical Commission

128. The Statistical Commission's primary aims are to promote the development of national statistics and the improvement of their comparability; co-ordinate the statistical work of Specialised Agencies and promote the improvement of statistics and statistical methods more generally. The UK has been a continuous member since its creation and is represented by the Office for National Statistics.

129. The Statistical Commission provides leadership and co-ordination for official statistics at a global level. It promotes the UN Fundamental Principles of Statistics and provides a forum for discussing longer-term issues.

130. The United Kingdom occupies a central position in providing technical assistance in the field of statistics. The Statistical Commission provides a forum for influencing professional colleagues across the world on development issues where quality statistics are vital for effective poverty monitoring and poverty reduction strategies.

131. During the last four years of membership the UK has played a key role in developing a range of statistical indicators. DFID has provided technical advice and financial support for work underpinning the choice of indicators to monitor progress towards the Millennium Development Goals.

Commission on Population and Development (CPD)

132. The UK was consistently a member of the Commission on Population and Development (CPD) between 1947 and 2001. Although the UK does not currently have a seat on the CPD, DFID is considering whether to run in the 2004 election for the term 2005-2008.

133. A notable success of UK observers and other donors involved in the 2003 Commission meeting was to avert a full blown International Conference on Population and Development (ICPD+10), proposed for 2004. Such a chapter-by-chapter review of the 1994 ICPD Programme of Action would have provided conservative states with another significant opportunity to seek to roll back internationally agreed language on sexual and reproductive health and rights, which the UK wishes to avoid.

Sustainable Development – Environment and Development

Commission on Sustainable Development (CSD)

134. The Commission on Sustainable Development (CSD) was established following the United Nations Conference on Environment and Development (UNCED) – the Rio "Earth Summit". In 2002 the World Summit on Sustainable Development (WSSD) in Johannesburg reviewed progress made over the previous decade.

135. WSSD reiterated CSD's role as a high level forum on sustainable development. It is tasked to:

- Review progress and elaborate policy guidance and options for future activities to achieve sustainable development, predominantly follow up at the international, regional and national levels of WSSD's Johannesburg Plan of Implementation (JPOI), and Agenda 21.

- Act as a focal point for action-orientated multi-stakeholder partnerships for sustainable development.

136. The UK has been a member of CSD since 1994 and has been elected for a further term until 2006. Given the wide-ranging nature of sustainable development, a number of UK Government Departments have an interest in CSD, with the DEFRA in the lead.

137. Heads of State and Government at WSSD agreed that a step change in CSD delivery is needed. In future CSD will organise itself into two-year action-orientated implementation cycles and a seven-cycle work programme of thematic clusters. The prioritisation of water, sanitation and human settlements as the thematic cluster for the 2004-5 cycle has underlined the importance of sustainable development for poverty eradication.

138. The CSD work programme also covers actions in developed countries, for example sustainable patterns of consumption and production; renewable energy and energy efficiency; managing and protecting our own natural resources and the positive and negative social, economic and environmental impacts of the developed world's consumption of global natural resources. There is particular emphasis on oceans and fisheries, biodiversity, forests and illegal logging, chemicals use and management.

139. The achievement of sustainable development is a major challenge for the international community, and will be a test of the capacity of the UN to deliver on behalf of the global collective, in the face of entrenched national interests. Much rides on the follow up to WSSD.

140. The CSD must remain focussed on implementation through reviewing progress, identifying barriers and offering solutions. There should be an emphasis on integrating the economic, social and environmental dimensions of sustainable development, in a balanced way in both developed and developing countries.

141. CSD will need to work with bodies such as UNEP, UNDP and the international financial institutions, backed up by continuing high-level commitment through the UN General Assembly and ECOSOC. HMG will continue work in a number of UN fora and processes to improve inter-agency co-ordination on WSSD follow-up, particularly encouraging joint working between UNEP and UNDP, as well as promoting integrated and coherent follow-up to WSSD, the Monterrey Financing for Development Conference and the Millennium Summit.

United Nations Environment Programme (UNEP)

142. The United Nations Environment Programme (UNEP) was established to promote international co-operation in the field of the environment, to provide policy guidance for the direction and co-ordination of UN environment programmes, and to keep the world environmental situation under review.

143. The 1997 Nairobi Declaration emphasised that UNEP should continue to be 'the leading global environmental authority that sets the global environmental agenda, that promotes the coherent implementation of the environmental dimensions of sustainable development within the United Nations system and that serves as an authoritative advocate for the global environment'. UNEP is also, with UNDP and the World Bank, one of three implementing agencies of the Global Environment Facility (GEF).

144. The UK is one of the 58 current members of the UNEP Governing Council (GC). The UK participates in the Governing Council and has a Permanent Mission to UNEP based in Nairobi. DEFRA lead on policy for HMG.

145. UNEP derives funding from the Environment Fund; UN Regular Budget and Trust Funds associated with specific activities. The UK seems likely to be the single largest Environment Fund contributor for 2003 giving £4.2 million, which represents approximately 10% of the budget. The UK contributed a further $10.59 million to Trust Funds in 2002, most of which funded the implementation of the Montreal Protocol.

146. UNEP alone cannot achieve the environmental outcomes and goals set out in the WSSD Plan of Implementation and Agenda 21. This requires global consensus and action at all levels: global, regional, national and local. It is important that UN agencies and programmes integrate environmental issues into their activities. UNEP, UNDP, CSD and the international financial institutions will need to work closely together for effective implementation.

147. In 2002 UNEP played an important role in setting the agenda for environmental aspects of WSSD. The UK's future priorities for UNEP include:

- To broaden the base of financial contributions to the Environment Fund and enhance the predictability, stability and flexibility of funding as a requirement for a strengthened institutional structure;

- To establish universal membership for the Governing Council/Global Ministerial Environmental Forum;

- To focus UNEP on its core normative environmental functions and promoting the environmental dimension of sustainable development within the UN system, with a strong emphasis on implementing WSSD outcomes;

- Work on chemicals, bio-diversity and sustainable consumption and production (SCP), regional sea agreements and land-based sources of marine pollution;

- Continued emphasis on UNEP's co-ordination with other elements of the UN structure to mainstream the environmental dimension of sustainable development.

United Nations Human Settlements Programme (UN-HABITAT)

148. UN-HABITAT based in Nairobi, formerly known as United Nations Centre for Human Settlements, is the lead UN agency for co-ordinating activities in the field of human settlements. It is the focal point for the implementation of the Habitat Agenda, the plan of action adopted at the Habitat II Conference in Istanbul in 1996. Its activities contribute to the overall objective of the UN system to reduce poverty, ensure the provision of adequate shelter and promote sustainable development within the context and the challenges of a rapidly urbanising world. The UN-HABITAT budget for 2002 is US$150 million. In 2002 the UK contributed £2.1 million, including a core contribution of £1 million.

149. Over the past 4 years, the UK has helped the agency undertake a fundamental rethink in respect of its role and its focus within the United Nations system. As a result of these efforts, the UK helped spearhead a revitalisation of the agency, culminating in the December 2001 decision of the UN General Assembly to upgrade the organisation to full UN programme status. The decision to focus on key issues – such as secure tenure and urban governance – has been instrumental in boosting the confidence of member states and the donor community alike in UN-HABITAT.

150. The UK plays a leading role on the Governing Council of UN-HABITAT. The UK role has focussed on implementing the objectives in DFID's UN-HABITAT Institutional Strategy Paper. These include:

- Supporting the revitalisation of UN-HABITAT to ensure that management practice and organisation is continually improved, finances are better managed and monitored, and confidence in the activities of the Programme is restored;

- Supporting specific efforts to provide a strategic focus on development issues, in particular the elimination of urban poverty, in the activities of the Centre;

- Supporting measures to reinforce UN-HABITAT's attempts to establish itself as a centre of excellence in the development and sharing of effective policies for sustainable human settlements and urban poverty reduction;

- Helping to develop effective indicators for monitoring the implementation of the Habitat Agenda and supporting efforts to turn the broad-based International Development Targets in the Habitat Global Plan of Action into agreed priorities and measurable targets for sustainable urban development and urban poverty reduction.

UN Forum on Forests (UNFF)

151. As a result of continuing pressure for a legally binding Convention on forests, the UN Forum on Forests (UNFF) was established to promote the implementation of the Forest Principles, the Intergovernmental Panel and the Intergovernmental Forum on Forests which emerged from the 1992 UN Conference on the Environment and Development. The UNFF aims to strengthen political commitment to sustainable forest management through Ministerial engagement, liaison with international and regional organisations, and the promotion of international policy.

152. The work of the UNFF is supported by the Collaborative Partnership on Forests (CPF) which facilitates co-operation and co-ordination amongst the key international institutions involved in forests, promotes adoption of the principles of sustainable forest management, and supports implementation. The CPF is chaired by the Food and Agriculture Organisation and is made up of the major international organisations and bodies involved in forests.

153. The work programme adopted in 2001 provides a framework for assessing progress towards implementation of forestry commitments, for highlighting best practice and for identifying challenges to the achievement of sustainable forest management. The UK believes that the priority for the UNFF should be implementation of forestry commitments, and that this would be best supported by focussing on national forest programmes, monitoring, assessment, reporting and financing. The UK wants to make the UNFF a more effective body and the primary focus for sustainable forest management within the UN system.

Health

World Health Organisation (WHO)

154. WHO is the main global health organisation and, as such, is key both to advancing the normative, standard-setting health agenda and in promoting health in the context of development. WHO has its Headquarters in Geneva, with six Regional Offices and

country offices in some member states. The Department of Health is the lead Government Department for WHO, while DFID also works closely with WHO and makes a major contribution. WHO is a UN Specialised Agency.

155. The UK's assessed contribution for the 2004-5 biennium will be around $51.1 million: around 5.45% of the WHO regular budget. In 2003 the UK's total extra-budgetary contributions were about £39 million, or about 8.6% of WHO's total annual budget.

156. The Department of Health recognises that WHO is particularly important in setting global norms and standards and leading the global response to health issues. WHO is key in leading global efforts on monitoring and surveillance of communicable disease, preparedness for incidents of biological, chemical or radiological release and vaccination and immunisation programmes.

157. DFID has set out its priorities for WHO in an Institutional Strategy Paper (ISP) which sets out how DFID will work with WHO to achieve the DFID White Paper objectives and the MDGs that are related to health and poverty. These priorities include strengthening the international and country presence of WHO, introducing a better alignment of human and financial resources with strategic objectives and programming, and ensuring WHO fully embraces the MDGs and poverty reduction.

158. The World Health Assembly (WHA), held in May each year, is the supreme decision-making body. The Executive Board (the governing body), comprises members qualified in the field of health designated by elected member states. The UK is currently a member of the Executive Board.

159. A recent WHO success was the adoption of the Framework Convention on Tobacco Control (FCTC) in May 2003. When the treaty comes into effect it will require Parties to undertake a total ban or severe restrictions on advertising and marketing, tough new rules on labelling, tougher action on smuggling and measures against passive smoking. This is regarded as a decisive benefit for securing domestic objectives for reducing tobacco consumption. The recent outbreak of SARS demonstrated the vital importance of WHO and international co-operation on health, as well as the potential effects of health incidents on economies.

Joint UN Programme on HIV/AIDS (UNAIDS)

160. By the mid-1990s, it became clear that the relentless spread of HIV, and the epidemic's devastating impact on all aspects of human lives, and social and economic development, were creating an emergency that would require a greatly expanded United Nations effort. No single United Nations organisation can provide the co-ordinated assistance needed to address the many factors driving the HIV epidemic or help countries deal with the impact of HIV/AIDS.

161. To address these challenges, the United Nations drew the relevant bodies together in a co-sponsored programme, the Joint United Nations Programme on HIV/AIDS (UNAIDS). The Joint Programme acts as the main advocate for world-wide action against HIV/AIDS and aims to lead, strengthen and support an expanded response to the epidemic. It has four goals:

 – To prevent the spread of HIV;

- To provide care and support for those infected and affected by the disease;

- To reduce the vulnerability of individuals and communities to HIV/AIDS;

- To alleviate the socio-economic and human impact of the epidemic.

162. With an annual budget of $250 million for the next biennium and a staff of 139 professionals, UNAIDS is a modest-sized programme with a substantial impact. The UNAIDS Secretariat operates as a catalyst and co-ordinator of action on AIDS, rather than as a direct funding or implementing agency. The UK core contribution is £3 million per annum. Total UK contributions are about 10.2% of the total budget.

163. UNAIDS aims to bring together the unique expertise, resources, and networks of influence that each of the composite organisations offers. Working together through UNAIDS, the co-sponsors expand their outreach through strategic alliances with other UN agencies, national governments, corporations, media, religious organisations, community groups, networks of people living with HIV/AIDS, and other NGOs. UNAIDS has been notably successful in this work.

Human Rights

164. The United Nations is the single most important body for promoting human rights worldwide. The Universal Declaration on Human Rights of 1948 provided the first globally accepted list of inalienable human rights. Since then, the United Nations has provided the framework for the international community to develop a sophisticated system of protection for human rights, based on legally binding treaties. The UK is a party to the six core human rights treaties. We take our obligations under them extremely seriously, including the obligation to provide regular reports to the bodies which monitor states' compliance with the treaties.

165. The UK is playing an active part in drawing up new human rights standards. The UK was one of the first countries to sign the Optional Protocol to the UN Convention Against Torture, which was adopted by the UN General Assembly in 2002 and provides for international monitoring of places of detention. The UK is an active participant in the work of a UN Ad Hoc Committee which is considering proposals for an International Convention on the Protection of the Rights and Dignity of People with Disabilities.

166. The UN Secretary-General's paper on UN reform "Strengthening the United Nations" re-asserted the sentiment in the UN Declaration on Human Rights, that human rights were central to all activities of the UN and its partners. The UK continues to pay particular regard to this in its relationships with the organisations of the UN.

United Nations Commission on Human Rights (CHR)

167. The UK attaches great importance to the work of the UN Commission on Human Rights (CHR), which is the main UN forum for discussion of human rights issues. The CHR's remit includes developing international human rights standards and addressing serious violations of human rights around the world. Its 53 member countries meet for six weeks in Geneva each spring. CHR resolutions establish UN Special Procedures (e.g. special rapporteurs, special representatives and working groups) and encourage the

Office of the UN High Commissioner for Human Rights (OHCHR) to focus on particular issues in the course of their work. The UK has been a member for all but two years since the CHR's inception in 1946.

168. Each year the EU tables a number of resolutions, for example on thematic issues such as the death penalty, as well as on the human rights situations in individual countries such as North Korea, Burma and Zimbabwe. Thematic resolutions at CHR play an important role in helping define and develop international human rights standards. Resolutions on individual countries can help constrain the extent of abuses, give encouragement to human rights defenders working in those countries and sometimes act as a stimulus for wider change.

169. The United Kingdom is committed to helping improve the output of the UN human rights system. At present, the debate is polarised, politicised and often out of touch with the realities of the human rights situation in many countries. Too many members of the Commission on Human Rights themselves have bad human rights records or fail to co-operate fully with the UN human rights mechanisms. The UK works to promote a constructive dialogue at CHR, while reinforcing the key principles that states have obligations to promote the human rights of their citizens, and that it is part of CHR's responsibility to call the worst offenders to account.

170. The UK has sympathy with those who argue that the UN should impose criteria for CHR membership, but such reform is unlikely to be agreed in the foreseeable future. And criteria would need to distinguish between those paying lip service to human rights by ratifying the main conventions, and those who are serious about implementing their obligations. We urge countries to use the spotlight of CHR membership as an opportunity to demonstrate their commitment to the UN human rights system by ratifying the key Conventions and co-operating with the CHR's mechanisms. Meanwhile, we will continue to work to ensure the CHR continues to address country-specific issues where the situation on the ground merits it. We believe that a CHR which concentrates solely on thematic issues without highlighting transgressors would be failing to fulfil its original mandate.

Office of the UN High Commissioner for Human Rights (OHCHR)

171. Under the leadership of the High Commissioner for Human Rights, the Office of the UN High Commissioner for Human Rights (OHCHR) supports the special procedures of the Commission on Human Rights and other appropriate UN bodies. It monitors human rights in field offices and provides technical assistance at the requests of governments in a number of countries. The Office assists the development of national human rights institutions and supports their participation at international fora. It supports UN treaty monitoring bodies – the committees that monitor the implementation of the six core UN human rights treaties. OHCHR is also responsible for fully integrating human rights in the work of the UN.

172. The UK has a strong partnership with OHCHR through an Institutional Strategy Paper (ISP). The UK is the second largest donor to the OHCHR in terms of voluntary contributions. From 2000-2002, the UK contributed nearly £8 million. The major objectives of our support are:

– To enhance the capacity of the OHCHR in order to support the development and management of its field programmes and operations;

- To mainstream all human rights across the work of the UN system;
- To integrate economic, social and cultural rights into the UN's work;
- To provide human rights information to other implementing agencies.

173. These priorities are consistent with the recommendations in "Strengthening of the United Nations". This report included four human rights recommendations: strengthening UN capacity to help countries build strong human rights institutions; reviewing the procedures of the treaty monitoring bodies to simplify reporting obligations; reviewing the special procedures system to make it more effective and better supported; and strengthening the management of the OHCHR. Through the regular review missions conducted by DFID, to both HQ and the field to evaluate and support progress, the UK has increasing confidence in OHCHR.

International Labour Organisation (ILO)

174. The International Labour Organisation (ILO) is the United Nations Specialised Agency which promotes internationally recognised rights for workers, primarily through Conventions that are legally binding on those countries which ratify them, and monitors how those rights are being applied. The ILO currently has 175 member states. The ILO's tripartite structure is unique for a UN body, with workers and employers participating as equal partners with governments.

175. The DWP meets the cost of the ILO subscription. The UK currently pays 5.45% of the total budget, which for 2003 is approximately £8.75 million. The UK is one of ten chief industrial states that are permanent titular members of the ILO Governing Body.

176. The UK's priorities are to ensure that the ILO produces effective, workable and widely ratifiable international instruments. The UK played a major role in negotiating the 1998 Declaration on Fundamental Principles and Rights at Work which provides a framework of international rights for workers, as set out in the ILO's core labour standards. These standards cover freedom of association and the right to collective bargaining; elimination of forced and child labour; and ending of discrimination in employment. The Declaration commits member states to respect and promote the ILO core labour standards whether or not they have ratified the relevant ILO Conventions. The UK has ratified the entire ILO core Conventions. The Government will continue to promote the ILO Declaration and will encourage all member states to ratify and implement the ILO core Conventions.

177. The UK also played a crucial role in negotiating ILO Convention 182 on the Elimination of the Worst Forms of Child Labour (1999) which is one of the 'core' ILO Conventions and has become widely ratified.

178. The UK has helped to increase the profile of employment issues on the ILO agenda and we ensured that the follow up to the World Summit on Social Development (Copenhagen, 2000) gave the ILO a mandate to develop a global employment strategy. We continue to stress the importance of jobs as the key route out of poverty.

179. Since 1997, DFID has supported ILO poverty-related activities at sectoral and country level. The initial focus of support has been on the elimination of child labour but support for other ILO programmes has increased. In response to the increasing

overlap of DFID's interests with those of ILO, it was agreed that the relationship should be drawn into a more coherent framework agreement. In April 2001, the Secretary of State for International Development approved a four-year, £15 million Partnership Framework. This enables the two organisations to develop shared objectives and priorities and to channel funds to selected work programmes.

Humanitarian

Office for the Co-ordination of Humanitarian Affairs (OCHA)

180. The overarching role of the Office for the co-ordination of humanitarian affairs (OCHA) is to mobilise and co-ordinate effective and principled humanitarian action in order to alleviate human suffering in disasters and emergency situations. It has no organisational authority over UN humanitarian operations, and its role is to bring coherence through the provision of a range of co-ordination services.

181. The Organisation's Headquarters are split between New York and Geneva. The New York Office co-ordinates humanitarian issues and develops humanitarian policy. Key functions of the Geneva Office include support for OCHA's field offices and management of the Inter-Agency Consolidated Appeals Process (CAP).

182. The UK is among OCHA's largest donors. Apart from funding under DFID's institutional partnership with OCHA, the UK supports OCHA through emergency responses and through geographical programmes.

183. DFID's institutional strategic partnership with OCHA, governed by an Institutional Strategy Paper (ISP), covered the 3 year period 1999/00 – 2001/02 and was tied to a provision of £3 million a year. A new four-year partnership agreement is presently under negotiation. Meanwhile OCHA have received "bridging finance" to enable them to continue with relevant strengthening activities.

184. The purpose of the partnership has been to improve the impact of OCHA's work through strengthening emergency response, policy development and management support. The new ISP will continue to embrace the core areas of OCHA's work and will also assist in strengthening information management capacity and communications technologies.

Office of the UN High Commissioner for Refugees (UNHCR)

185. The Office of the United Nations High Commissioner for Refugees (UNHCR) is mandated to lead and co-ordinate international action to protect refugees and resolve refugee problems throughout the world. Its primary purpose is to safeguard the rights and well being of refugees.

186. The international obligation to provide protection for refugees arises from the 1951 Refugee Convention. UNHCR was set up to oversee implementation of the Convention, and individual signatories have the primary responsibility for protecting refugees. In the UK, the Home Office is responsible for implementing our obligations under the 1951 Convention through the asylum system, and it works closely with UNHCR in doing so.

187. The UK provides support to UNHCR to strengthen its capacity to protect refugees through enhancement of its response to emergencies, programme planning and delivery, accountability mechanisms and working relationships with key stakeholders. UNHCR makes a strong contribution to our aim of reducing loss of life and livelihood in emergencies.

188. The UK's contribution to UNHCR in 2002 was £21.4 million. We work with the UNHCR through a mutually agreed Institutional Strategy Paper, and monitor this through an annual review and attendance at Standing Committees. The UK attends the Executive Council and Standing Committees of the UNHCR.

189. UK priorities are:

- To strengthen UNHCR's capacity to respond to emergencies and improve safety and security for staff and operations;

- To enhance the quality of UNHCR's programme planning and delivery;

- To strengthen the governance and accountability of UNHCR;

- To encourage UNHCR to develop stronger working partnerships with key stakeholders.

190. Recent successes include returning Angolan refugees from Zambia, establishing protection for Afghan refugees and facilitating their return when it is possible to do so in safety and dignity. UNHCR is providing assistance to the most vulnerable among the 350,000 refugees from Croatia and Bosnia and Herzegovina who are presently living in Serbia and Montenegro. In Kosovo they are creating the conditions conducive to the safe and sustainable return of minorities.

World Food Programme (WFP)

191. The World Food Programme (WFP) is the food aid arm of the United Nations system. It is the largest humanitarian agency in the world, with a budget in 2002 of over $3 billion. Food aid is one of the many instruments that can help to promote food security. The UK believes that WFP food aid must be oriented towards eradicating hunger and poverty.

192. About 85% of WFP's food aid is used to meet emergency and rehabilitation needs and 15% to support economic and social development amongst the most vulnerable people in developing countries. WFP provides important logistical support both to get food aid to the right people at the right time and in support of other UN and Non-Governmental Organisation humanitarian operations.

193. The UK is one of WFP's largest donors. In 2002 the UK contributed over £65 million, mostly to humanitarian operations. So far in 2003, UK contributions have slightly exceeded this amount, including £33 million for the programme in Iraq.

194. The UK provides support to WFP through a partnership to strengthen its institutional capacity and improve its food aid interventions. The partnership has four objectives:

- Strengthen WFP capacity to respond to emergencies;

- Enhance the quality of programme management;

- Greater use of sustainable livelihoods approaches in WFP programming;

- Strengthen governance and accountability of WFP.

195. The partnership is worth £20 million over 4 years. The UK also promotes better policies and operations through the Executive Board (of which the UK Permanent Representative to Rome is currently President) and by strengthening co-operation at country level.

Office of the United Nations Security Co-ordinator (UNSECOORD)

196. The Office of the UN Security Co-ordinator (UNSECOORD) is the key UN body for countering the growing trend of attacks against civilian humanitarian field workers. DFID contributed £1 million to UNSECOORD in 2002, to help the organisation deal with the threat to UN staff and secondees. In addition, DFID works directly with UNSECOORD on operational issues and in 2001/2 DFID undertook a six-month review study of UN relief agencies security and made recommendations for improvements.

UN Relief and Works Agency for Palestinian Refugees (UNRWA)

197. Following the 1948 Arab-Israeli war, the United Nations Relief and Works Agency for Palestine Refugees in the Near East (UNRWA) was established to carry out direct relief and works programmes for Palestine refugees. Today, UNRWA is the main provider of basic services – education, health, relief and social services – to over 3.9 million registered Palestine refugees in the Middle East (West Bank & Gaza Strip, Jordan, Syria and Lebanon).

198. UNRWA operations are financed almost entirely by voluntary contributions from Governments, which account for 95% of all income. The regular operations budget (excluding Emergency Appeals) for 2003 is just over $300 million.

199. The UK supports UNRWA's work to alleviate the plight of Palestinian refugees, which is a key issue for the success of the Middle East Peace Process. We have provided core funding for UNRWA since its creation. Over the last five years we have sought to develop a positive and productive partnership that encourages UNRWA to increase its efficiency and effectiveness. UK annual contributions have risen commensurately, reaching almost £22 million in 2002. The UK is now UNRWA's second largest bilateral donor.

Crime and Justice

UN Commission on Crime Prevention and Criminal Justice

200. The UN Commission on Crime Prevention and Criminal Justice discusses a wide range of international crime issues. The UK will take a seat on the Commission from January 2004. The Home Office is the UK Lead Department.

201. The Commission oversees the Centre for International Crime Prevention, including the management of the UN Crime Prevention and Criminal Justice Fund, which provides technical assistance and advisory services to member states, including

in the areas of transnational organised crime, terrorism and reconstruction of criminal justice systems. In 2002 the United Kingdom provided contributions of $298,659 to the Fund, out of total contributions amounting to $5.01 million.

202. The UK values the contribution made by the Commission especially in the fight against organised and international crime, financial crime and corruption and in promoting effective co-operation between police and judicial authorities. The UK supported the proposal for a UN Convention against transnational organised crime (UNTOC) which was initially discussed in the Crime Commission. The UK signed the Convention, which provides for international co-operation to combat organised crime, in December 2000. The UK has also signed Protocols to the Convention dealing with migrant smuggling, trafficking in persons and trafficking in firearms.

203. The Commission has helped to develop a proposal for a UN Convention against Corruption (UNCAC). Negotiations in an ad hoc committee should be completed in the near future. UNCAC will cover Definitions, Prevention, Criminalisation, Monitoring and Implementation. The UK stresses the importance of preventative measures against corruption and we have succeeded in influencing the content of UNCAC in this respect.

UN Commission on Narcotic Drugs (CND)

204. The Commission on Narcotic Drugs (CND) is the central UN policy-making body dealing with drug-related matters. It analyses the world drug situation, develops proposals to strengthen the international drug control system and is the custodian of the three UN Conventions that form the basis of international and national drug control. The UK has been a member of CND since 1947. The UK has a number of specific interests in the CND, in particular:

- UN Conventions: A principal object of the Conventions that the Commission administers is to make available sufficient narcotic drugs and psychotropic substances for medical and scientific purposes. The UK has one of the world's leading pharmaceutical industries so it is important that we are represented on an international body that controls the availability of its raw materials;

- Drugs Policy: Since UK accession to all three international drugs treaties means that our domestic drugs laws and policies must follow their lead, our membership of CND means we are in a position where we can influence international policy in this area;

- UN Reform: At the last CND the UK tabled and pushed through a resolution on management, calling upon the Executive Director to press forward with his programme of reform with a focus on the UK priorities of improving project management skills and introducing an evaluation function.

UN Office on Drugs and Crime

205. The CND governs the drug-related activities and funds of the UN Office on Drugs and Crime (UNODC). The UK has consistently been among the four or five largest donors to UNODC. The UK donated £4.2 million in 2002, about 11% of total voluntary contributions to the organisation. These funds are to support projects that the UK could not undertake alone, either due to a lack of capacity or because they require the sort of legitimacy that only an international body can bring (e.g. the UNODC poppy survey in Afghanistan).

206. The UK funds UNODC projects that support UK objectives and complement our own bilateral activity. As lead nation on counter narcotics in Afghanistan, we work particularly closely with the UNODC office in Kabul and are involved in joint activities there. We have also recently supported activity in Colombia, the Eastern Caribbean, Peru, Iran, South East Europe and Central Asia.

Transport and Meteorological

International Civil Aviation Organisation (ICAO)

207. The International Civil Aviation Organisation (ICAO) is a Specialised UN Agency, with a membership of 188 states. Its task is to produce, update, and promulgate Resolutions, Guidance, Standards and Recommended Practices which, if followed by all the contracting states, help to ensure safe and fair operation of air traffic around the world. The UK has held a seat on the Governing Council since the Organisation was founded under the Chicago Convention of 1944. The UK Delegation office in Montreal is the main interface between the UK and ICAO.

208. Global standards and recommended practices stemming from ICAO, prepared with active UK participation, and reflecting UK practice and experience, enable the international aviation industry to continue growing, and help the UK maintain its prominent position in the industry. In addition to the key objective of improving aviation safety, there is a range of programmes (notably with satellite navigation systems, in achieving increasingly high standards of security and in setting environmental rules) which provide commercial opportunities for UK firms.

209. The UK regards the Universal Safety Oversight Audit Programme (USOAP) as the most important ICAO programme to be initiated in many years. International aviation operates on the basis that each Contracting State of ICAO is responsible for the safety oversight of its own aircraft, operators and personnel, and will accept aircraft from other states flying over or into its territory provided they meet minimum standards set down by ICAO. However, it became apparent some time ago that some states do not have the resources and/or the expertise to guarantee adequate safety oversight. ICAO responded by developing what has become a universal, effectively mandatory, programme of safety oversight audits.

210. The UK's contribution is currently 5.3% of the total budget, amounting in 2003 to more than £1.7 million, making the UK the 5th largest contributor.

International Maritime Organisation (IMO)

211. The International Maritime Organisation (IMO) is the UN Specialised Agency devoted exclusively to international maritime issues. Initially the IMO was established to address maritime safety issues, but soon extended its remit to include the protection of the marine environment.

212. There are currently 162 member states, three Associate Members and nearly 100 Inter-Governmental Organisations that have concluded agreements of co-operation with IMO or Non-Governmental Organisations in Consultative Status with IMO. The UK is a Category A member of the IMO Council, i.e. one of the ten states with the largest interest in providing international shipping services.

36

213. The IMO is considered one of the most successful of the UN Specialised Agencies in terms of the ratification rate of its principal Conventions. For example, the International Convention on the Safety of Life at Sea (SOLAS), 1974 and its Protocol of 1978 has been ratified by states that represent approximately 95% of the world fleet.

214. The IMO is the only UN Specialised Agency to have its headquarters in the UK, on the Albert Embankment in London. The Department for Transport (DfT) owns the building and undertakes landlord duties and is also responsible for paying the UK's annual subscription. UK contributions for the biennium 2002-2003 totalled £1.4 million (3.4% of the total budget).

215. In addition, the UK government has signed a Memorandum of Understanding with the IMO to support the Organisation's technical co-operation activities. From March 2000 we have agreed to contribute £40,000 per annum for five years. We are also currently providing £100,000 per annum towards the funding of the World Maritime University based in Sweden.

216. The Maritime and Coastguard Agency (MCA) and the Department for Transport (DfT) are lead Departments for the IMO. In addition the DfT, DEFRA, FCO, Customs and Excise, Immigration, Health and Safety Executive (HSE) and the UK Hydrographic Office also provide policy advice. The UK has supported an on-going strategic review of the organisation.

217. Under the chairmanship of the UK, the Maritime Safety Committee at its meeting in December 2002 adopted amendments to the SOLAS convention to include new maritime security requirements in light of the events of September 11th. These amendments will enter into force and apply to more than 95% of the world fleet on 1 July 2004.

World Meteorological Organisation (WMO)

218. For the Met Office to maintain its global numerical weather prediction capability – which enables it to forecast the weather both at home and for UK military commitments overseas – it requires real-time observational data of the atmosphere and ocean from around the world. The WMO World Weather Watch (WWW) Programme co-ordinates both the taking of upper-air, surface and satellite measurements by all its Members, and the telecommunication infrastructure necessary to distribute this data to all Members in real-time.

219. Observations are also required for detecting climate change and assessing the Met Office climate model used to predict the future climate under different greenhouse gas emissions scenarios. WMO helps co-ordinate climate observations through the inter-agency Global Climate Observing System (GCOS), and the monitoring of greenhouse gas concentrations through the Global Atmospheric Watch.

220. The Met Office is the lead UK Department for this Specialised Agency. The Chief Executive of the Met Office is currently the UK Permanent Representative to WMO. In 2002 the UK contribution to WMO, paid by the Met Office, was £2,024 million, of which £612,000 were voluntary contributions and £1,412,000 were assessed contributions. The assessed contributions comprised 5.5% of the WMO regular budget.

221. The main UK priority is seeking to improve the efficiency and effectiveness of the organisation and ensuring that its activities continue to provide the benefits described above. This is achieved by active participation in WMO meetings at all levels (Congress, Executive Council, and Technical Commissions) to ensure that:

- the scientific and technical programmes progress in the interest of the UK;

- the organisation embraces administrative and structural reform.

222. The United Nations Framework Convention on Climate Change (UNFCCC) provides the international framework for global efforts to tackle climate change. The Kyoto Protocol, which sets legally binding targets to cut or limit greenhouse gas emissions and is perhaps the most ambitious Multilateral Environmental Agreement ever, falls under the UNFCCC. The UK contributed 5.36% of the UNFCCC core budget of £10.4 million in 2003 (UK share of approximately £550,000) and also contributed a further £300,000 in voluntary contributions.

Industry, Energy and Communications

International Atomic Energy Agency (IAEA)

223. The UK is a significant contributor to the International Atomic Energy Agency's (IAEA) activities. The UK's largest annual financial contribution is to the Agency's regular budget. This budget funds the Agency's core programmes, which include nuclear safety, nuclear security and verification activities. The current assessed rate for the UK is 5.5%, which amounted to £8 million in 2003. The UK is a designated Member of the Agency's Board of Governors, which meets regularly throughout the year.

224. The Agency has three main areas of activity: nuclear safety, nuclear safeguards and technical co-operation. Technical co-operation is used to promote the peaceful use of nuclear energy and is a key feature of the Agency's work for developing countries. The UK makes a significant annual voluntary contribution towards the Agency's Technical Co-operation Fund (currently £2.5 million per annum).

225. The UK maintains a Member State Support Programme (MSSP), with an annual budget of about £1 million, to assist the IAEA in ensuring the continued and improved effectiveness of its safeguards system. In addition, extra-budgetary funding of about £90,000 per annum is provided to support IAEA travel and subsistence associated with UKSP tasks. The UK is also a major contributor to efforts to bring about change within the Agency. We contributed £75,000 towards a management consultancy for the Agency in 2002 and we have pledged a further offer of £100,000 this year for follow-up work.

226. Key priorities for the UK are nuclear security and compliance by states with their NPT and Agency safeguards obligations. Under the Nuclear Non-Proliferation Treaty, states parties are required to have a Comprehensive Safeguards Agreement (CSA) with the Agency in force. They are also encouraged to agree and implement an Additional Protocol to their CSA allowing for a more rigorous inspection system

227. The Agency's safeguards activities are key to deterring and detecting whether fissile material is being diverted to undeclared nuclear programmes. It essentially underpins the national nuclear counter-proliferation activities undertaken not only in this country, but also by many countries around the world.

228. The UK has long been concerned about the under-funded Safeguards Department, especially in the light of warnings last year by the Director General that without additional resources the Agency would no longer be able to guarantee credible safeguards. The UK has lobbied hard for the agreement of a significant budget increase in favour of safeguards activities. July 2003 saw agreement to an increased budget which now goes to the September General Conference for final approval.

229. Since September 11th, the threat of nuclear terrorism has become a prominent and increasingly important part of the Agency's agenda. The IAEA instigated a programme to promote activities to counter this threat. In 2002 the UK pledged £750,000 over three years to the Agency's Nuclear Security Fund.

International Telecommunication Union (ITU)

230. The fundamental reason for UK interest in the International Telecommunication Union (ITU), a UN Specialised Agency, relates to its role in maintaining the International Radio Regulations, an international treaty on the use of the frequency spectrum and satellite orbit. These decisions are of strategic and economic importance to the UK.

231. The Department for Trade and Industry takes the lead in ITU, but other Government Departments also have an interest. A number of telecommunications companies are UK Sector Members of ITU. The UK Member State financial contribution to ITU will reduce from 15 units (£2 million per annum) to 10 units (£1.3 million per annum) in January 2004. The UK contribution is approximately 2% of the total ITU budget.

232. UK specific objectives are therefore to:

- Create new spectrum allocations in line with UK policy (e.g. identification of 3G expansion bands, introduction of flexible allocations in TV bands);

- Defend existing allocations and assignments against threats from other countries (e.g. protection of heavily used fixed link bands, defence radar allocations);

- Harmonise allocations, licensing, technical standards and planning parameters where such harmonisation would be beneficial to the UK;

- Improve the management, structure and efficiency of the organisation;

- Ensure ITU restricts itself to the policy issues where global intergovernmental rule setting and regulation is appropriate and avoids involvement in areas where self regulatory or other lighter touch solutions would be more effective.

233. The main contribution of the ITU is its role as the only world-wide body that regulates the use of the frequency spectrum. Agreement in ITU is necessary to satisfy demand for new spectrum, protect existing services, reduce equipment costs, increase spectrum utilisation and provide internationally available services.

United Nations Industrial Development Organisation (UNIDO)

234. UNIDO is a small UN Specialised Agency based in Vienna with a mandate to promote sustainable industrial development on a global basis. UNIDO is increasingly focussing on its vision that sustained productivity gains are the key determinate of sustainable and equitable development.

235. UNIDO has a regular budget of around $65 million which is financed through the assessed contributions of 169 member states of which the UK's contribution is $3 million. UNIDO's technical co-operation delivery is in the order of $85 million per annum, which is financed from voluntary contributions. The UK contributed over $500,000 in 2002.

236. The UK recognises the key role of the private sector in driving the process of economic growth, an essential condition for poverty elimination. We are therefore committed to developing partnerships with business, both to help develop a strong private sector, and to work with the private sector in promoting growth patterns that are environmentally friendly and help contribute to international development goals. UNIDO, a member of the UN Global Compact, is a key partner in these areas.

237. One of our notable successes with UNIDO in recent years has been support for a management skills development programme for key UNIDO staff at HQ and country level. This has enabled UNIDO staff to develop leading-edge skills in organisational, staff and financial management. We have also funded a significant project on Results Based Management.

238. The UK is an influential member of UNIDO's Governing Board. Current objectives for the organisation are set out in DFID's Institutional Strategy Paper for UNIDO, which include:

- Increasing linkages between sustainable industrial development and poverty reduction;

- Encouraging and supporting UNIDO to focus on its areas of comparative advantage;

- Helping UNIDO to build its relationships with other UN agencies, and to participate in wider donor co-ordination activities.

Universal Postal Union (UPU)

239. The Universal Postal Union (UPU) is a Specialised Agency of the United Nations and the primary forum for co-operation between postal services to ensure a truly global postal network across its 189 member countries. It sets the legal and operational framework for international mail exchanges through its Acts and Regulations. It acts as a forum for the exchange of best practice, develops postal standards and encourages countries to improve the quality of service for customers.

240. The Department for Trade and Industry, with support from the Royal Mail and the FCO, represents the interests of the United Kingdom and the Overseas Territories. The UK's annual contributions to the budget are around £928,000 (6.2% of the total).

241. The UK also contributes through direct support for projects the UPU undertakes, especially providing experts for project work or additional financial resources. The UK is recognised for its regulatory reform of its postal market, and its active contribution to many aspects of the work of the UPU.

242. The UK holds a number of positions of responsibility and actively participates in a wide range of Working Groups. The UPU is currently undergoing a period of reform in an attempt to adapt to the fast changing patterns in the postal sector, commercialisation of the public postal operators and market liberalisation. The UK will continue to work actively to persuade the UPU, and its members, of the benefits of market reform and customer focus.

World Intellectual Property Organisation (WIPO)

243. The World Intellectual Property Organisation (WIPO) is the Specialised Agency responsible for administering international treaties and registration systems relating to patents, trademarks, designs, copyright, and other areas of Intellectual Property (IP). It facilitates discussion, reform, and harmonisation of IP policies and laws. It is also responsible for providing technical assistance to developing countries, and carries out awareness-raising activities in all member states.

244. The lead UK Department is the Patent Office (DTI). The UK contributes 1,1 million Swiss Francs annually to WIPO (normally around £500,000-£600,000). Contributions by member states make up a very small part of WIPO's income (around 6%), with the UK's contribution amounting to around 0.3%. Most of WIPO's considerable income comes from fees for the various registration systems it administers.

245. The UK priorities for WIPO are to ensure that its treaties and intellectual property registration systems reflect UK and, where appropriate, European, policies in relation to intellectual property. They should operate as a tool to stimulate innovation in the UK, whilst taking into account broader issues, such as the effect of patents on public health and access to essential medicines in developing countries. We aim to ensure that the technical assistance given by WIPO to developing countries is delivered in a balanced manner, appropriate to the specific needs of the country concerned, and is not merely concerned with pushing stronger IP protection systems onto the country.

246. The UK was recently successful in bringing forward a quality framework for patent offices across the world, which carry out work on international patent applications under the Patent Co-operation Treaty (PCT). The framework will provide assurance of the quality of this work, so that both the users of the patent system and other patent offices can use the results of this work with confidence, increasing the efficiency of national and international patent systems.

IV VISIONS FOR THE FUTURE: REFORMING THE UN

247. The United Nations has shown itself to be remarkably adaptable. Four times as many states are members as at its founding in the aftermath of the Second World War. It has responded to the great changes in the world of the last half-century: decolonisation; the end of the Cold War and the new challenges of the environment, AIDS, weapons of mass destruction and civil conflict.

248. Like any large organisation the UN needs to remain dynamic through a process of continuous change and adaptation. The British Government believes that this autumn's General Assembly represents an excellent opportunity to give this process a further push forward. In particular, there is a recognition that the General Assembly is under-performing, with many repetitive and sterile debates and resolutions. This view is shared by a number of other member states, from various different regional groups; and the new President of the General Assembly, Julian Hunte, has also signalled his intentions to carry forward reform. A relatively modest programme of reform of the General Assembly could allow it to regain the status it has lost as the only representative body of all international opinion, able to articulate the views of the international community. It is also right to give further support now to the Secretary-General's attempts to reform the Secretariat and budgetary processes. With three years of his second term remaining, Kofi Annan enjoys unrivalled prestige as Secretary-General, which presents an important opportunity to forward his reform agenda. His 2002 proposals "Strengthening of the United Nations: An agenda for further change" are a critical tool in achieving reform during his second term.

249. Against that background, we intend to continue our push for reform of the UN's institutions. In doing so we recognise the need to adopt approaches that differ significantly from those of the past.

250. No single member state or group of member states can drive any process of change. We shall aim to work with like-minded partners right across the UN system.

251. In the same spirit we have a particular role to play in bringing together the member states of the European Union and the United States, since the United Nations will not flourish without the full-hearted engagement of both.

252. It continues to be important – increasingly so – to reach out to civil society (whose importance in the world today is much greater than in 1945). This means working to improve the terms of access to UN bodies by NGOs in particular improving access to the General Assembly. In turn, this will mean developing criteria for NGO access to the UN to ensure that those NGOs who gain access are legitimate representatives of civil society. NGOs need assistance in building the expertise to interact with UN bodies, sometimes in new and innovative formations. We aim to work with others to foster this. The current Eminent Persons Panel, set up by the Secretary-General to consider the issue of civil society involvement with the UN, will receive £75,000 from DFID.

General Assembly

253. Any process of reform needs to focus hard on the General Assembly. It remains the only global organ in the institution, where all states – rich and poor, large and small, developed and developing – are represented. But its agenda and working methods continue to reflect the patterns of the Cold War era and the North-South divide. Too much of its business is repetitive and sterile and too much is conducted on the traditional bloc-by-bloc basis with the West on one side and the G77 developing countries on the other.

254. There is currently significant debate about how the General Assembly could be revitalised, involving a range of member states and the Secretariat. The incoming President of the General Assembly has indicated his desire to pursue new ideas. The UK

will support him in these efforts, as well as putting forward our own proposals. "Sunset clauses" should be introduced on resolutions and programmes that have served their purpose. Issues that do not need discussions every year should be bi-ennialised or tri-ennialised. This should equally be considered for other organs of the UN in New York, Geneva and elsewhere.

Secretariat

255. To complement efforts to reform the General Assembly it is essential to support the efforts of the Secretary-General to reform the Secretariat. His proposals of 2002 deserve continued serious consideration and implementation. The UN Secretariat's abilities and energy need to be harnessed by ensuring that all appointments are made on merit, and that there is equal access to jobs through initiatives such as targeted training, the funding of internship programmes, and support to graduates, particularly from developing countries, in finding the work experience that will qualify them to apply for UN posts. Systems of appraisal need to be further improved, ensuring the assessment of everyone's performance (up to the very highest level) against published criteria. The tendency for short-term contracts, making it harder to develop an independent civil service cadre, also requires attention. This process may also require a fresh look at term limits for all senior posts where two four-year terms are usually a sensible limit. The UK and other member states should also do more to look ahead to organising key senior appointments to ensure that the best candidates are attracted – and appointed.

The Development Architecture

256. The United Nations plays a key role in the international development architecture, along with other multilateral donors and bilateral donors. Reform started by the UN Secretary General in 1997 aimed to improve co-ordination of the UN family at country level, through instruments such as the Common Country Assessment (CCA), UN Development Assistance Framework (UNDAF) and the Common Services initiative. The UNDAF has been subsequently identified as the UN business plan for supporting country-owned Poverty Reduction Strategies (PRS) where they exist. DFID has provided support for this overall process.

257. A key part of the Secretary-General's 2002 reform proposals is his report on the "role and responsibilities in the provision of Technical Co-operation by UN entities" (expected in September 2003). In parallel with these efforts, individual UN bodies in the development area have launched ambitious programmes to improve human resource management, develop results-based management systems, identify core business and comparative advantage, and exit from peripheral activities.

258. DFID is currently developing a vision for the future of the UN development system, which is intended to help support the Secretary-General's reforms and to help inform our partnership with UN development agencies in the fight against global poverty. The vision is likely to emphasise the importance of continued progress toward internal coherence of the UN system at country level, and the integration of UN agency actions with those of other development partners. It will support an increased focus of our joint efforts on achievement of the Millennium Development Goals, in alignment with national poverty reduction strategies where they exist. We see scope for continued improvement in country level effectiveness of the UN system and will consider whether, alongside like-minded partners and others, we can use financial incentives to help achieve this.

Security Council

259. Just as there is debate about how the General Assembly should be revitalised, so there is significant debate about the functioning of the Security Council. The United Kingdom remains committed to a Security Council that is representative of the modern world, efficient and transparent. We have contributed to the improvement of the Council's working methods over the last few years. Successive UK Presidencies of the Council have promoted a more pro-active and transparent approach to involving the wider UN membership in the Council's work. We continue to believe that the Council should expand, with new permanent members who represent the regional realities of the modern world. There should also be expansion in the non-permanent membership of the Council to allow greater representation by the developing world. The expansion of the Council should be matched by a continued re-examination of its working methods. In particular, the Council should take steps to ensure that its working methods are adequate to deal with its extraordinarily busy and still expanding agenda.

Co-ordination

260. We need to support efforts to make the various parts of the United Nations play to their strengths; and co-ordinate their activities with those of other programmes and, where appropriate, specialised agencies. The Economic and Social Council needs to become more effective at co-ordinating the work of all the UN's bodies in the economic, sustainable development, humanitarian, human rights and social spheres. We need better co-ordination of the spectrum of activities from armed conflict prevention through peacekeeping to peace building and to ensure that the UN's peacekeeping capacity is meshed in with the activities of those of its member states. This can include developing a permanent African peacekeeping force, as envisaged by the G8, to working through ESDP to create an EU rapid reaction force for UN purposes. Such arrangements will need durable funding to underpin them. The UN and its member states also need to be more imaginative in examining the criteria for intervention in conflict situations. This will mean looking again at the recent work on humanitarian intervention; and it will mean examining issues that are not yet on the UN's agenda but where the threat of conflict is real.

261. In pursuing this we shall be guided by the link which the Secretary-General has made between conflict prevention, sustainable development and the Millennium Development Goals. Sustainable development is a key element of the overarching framework for UN activities, in particular for achieving the MDGs. More integrated and coherent follow-up of the outcomes of the major UN conferences, including the Millennium Summit, Monterrey and WSSD, will be an important aspect of UN reform. The prize is more effective and efficient multilateral action to tackle global poverty and environmental degradation.

New Threats

262. The UN must rise to meet the new threats facing the world in the 21st century. The work of the Security Council's Counter-Terrorism Committee established under UK chairmanship in the wake of the events of 11th September has reached an important juncture. We need to consider whether changes are needed that would enhance the profile of this work and help the Committee maintain the most dynamic approach to fulfilling its mandate. We are considering whether it should evolve into a professional and more independent agency with a strengthened staff of dedicated experts.

The United Kingdom's Engagement

263. Finally, it is essential to ensure that the engagement of the United Kingdom goes wider than that of the Government. We want to continue to engage the Civil Society and private sector, and to encourage well informed debate in Parliament. To that end we are proposing an annual Commons debate on the United Nations, probably timed to contribute to the preparation for each autumn's General Assembly. The first such debate will be on 11 September this year.

ANNEX

1. UK FINANCIAL CONTRIBUTIONS TO THE UN IN 2002

A. *UK Assessed Contributions to UN System* (£)		*Funding Dept*
World Heritage Fund	£137,349	DCMS
Basel Convention	£137,772	DEFRA
Biodiversity Convention	£325,457	DEFRA
Bonn Convention on Migratory Species (CMS)	£143,451	DEFRA
CMS – African-Eurasian Migratory Waterbirds Agreement (AEWA)	£120,282	DEFRA
CMS – Agreement on the Conservation of Bats in Europe (EUROBATS)	£474,434	DEFRA
CMS – Agreement on the Conservation of Cetaceans (ASCOBANS)	£21,169	DEFRA
Convention on Biological Diversity	£511,000	DEFRA
Convention on International Trade in Endangered Species	£144,323	DEFRA
Framework Convention on Climate Change	£474,434	DEFRA
Montreal Convention	£84,706	DEFRA
Ramsar Convention	£77,314	DEFRA
UNECE Convention on Long-Range Trans-Boundary Air Pollution	£180,000	DEFRA
Vienna Convention	£35,120	DEFRA
Food and Agriculture Organisation	£11,702,064	DFID
UN Educational Scientific and Cultural Organisation	£12,182,445	DFID
UN Industrial Development Organisation	£2,273,667	DFID
International Civil Aviation Organisation	£1,869,282	DfT
World Health Organisation	£15,719,301	DOH
International Atomic Energy Agency	£7,459,727	DTI
Universal Postal Union	£963,310	DTI
International Labour Organisation	£9,153,009	DWP
International Criminal Tribunal for Rwanda	£3,782,043	FCO
International Criminal Tribunal for Yugoslavia	£4,681,322	FCO
International Seabed Authority (UNCLOS)	£200,886	FCO
International Tribunal for the Law of the Sea (UNCLOS)	£387,356	FCO
Permanent Court of Arbitration	£14,290	FCO
UN Disengagement Observer Force (UNDOF)	£1,699,827	FCO
UN Interim Force in Lebanon (UNIFIL)	£2,639,604	FCO
UN Interim Mission in Kosovo (UNMIK)	£2,904,913	FCO
UN Iraq-Kuwait Observer Mission (UNIKOM)	£806,004	FCO
UN Mission for the Referendum in Western Sahara (MINURSO)	£2,330,227	FCO
UN Mission in Bosnia Herzegovina (UNMIBH)	£946,459	FCO
UN Mission in Ethiopia and Eritrea (UNMEE)	£9,038,451	FCO
UN Mission in Sierra Leone (UNAMSIL)	£28,331,513	FCO
UN Mission of Support in East Timor (UNMISET)	£11,647,340	FCO
UN Observer Mission in Georgia (UNOMIG)	£951,450	FCO
UN Organisation Mission on the Democratic Republic of Congo (MONUC)	£23,765,049	FCO
UN Peacekeeping Force in Cyprus (UNFICYP)	£933,997	FCO
United Nations Regular Budget	£43,119,892	FCO
World Meteorological Organisation	£1,412,000	MET Office
World Intellectual Property Organisation	£469,654	Patent Office
TOTAL	**£204,251,894**	

B. UK Voluntary Contributions to UN System (£)		Funding Dept
Biodiversity Convention	£185,543	DEFRA
Convention on Migratory Species (CMS)	£30,199	DEFRA
CMS – African-Eurasian Migratory Waterbirds Agreement (AEWA)	£22,103	DEFRA
CMS – Agreement on the Conservation of Bats in Europe (EUROBATS)	£61,435	DEFRA
CMS – Agreement on the Conservation of Cetaceans (ASCOBANS)	£60,000	DEFRA
Convention on International Trade in Endangered Species	£70,000	DEFRA
International Consultative Group on Food Irradiation	£3,000	DEFRA
Ramsar Convention	£25,000	DEFRA
UNFCCC Trust Fund for Developing Country Participation	£100,000	DEFRA
UNFCCC Trust Fund for Supplementary Activities	£10,000	DEFRA
Food and Agriculture Organisation	£5,849,443	DFID
Global Environment Facility	£20,549,000	DFID
International Fund for Agricultural Development	£3,717,662	DFID
International Labour Organisation	£3,291,118	DFID
International Labour Organisation	£101,550	DfT
International Labour Organisation	£392,720	DWP
UN AIDS	£7,073,440	DFID
UN Centre for Human Settlements (UN-HABITAT)	£2,094,535	DFID
UN Children's Fund	£44,190,285	DFID
UN Commission on the Status of Women support for expert group meeting	£10,000	DFID
UN Conference on Trade and Development	£733,282	DFID
UN Development Fund for Women	£5,109,362	DFID
UN Development Programme	£72,774,962	DFID
UN Education, Scientific and Cultural Organisation	£2,875,976	DFID
UN Population Fund	£22,362,797	DFID
UN High Commissioner for Refugees	£27,844,254	DFID
UN Industrial Development Organisation	£285,910	DFID
UN Mine Action Service	£4,713,000	DFID
UN Office for the Co-ordination of Humanitarian Affairs	£5,713,082	DFID
UN Office of the High Commissioner for Human Rights	£3,834,547	DFID
UN Relief and Works Agency	£21,846,121	DFID
UN Research Institute for Social Development	£100,000	DFID
World Bank, UNDP, UNEP Global Environment Facility	£2,569,818	DFID
World Health Organisation	£50,709,374	DFID

(continued on next page)

World Food Programme	£65,071,818	DFID
International Maritime Organisation	£140,000	DfT
Conversion of UK Nuclear Publications to INIS Database	£2,669	DTI
IAEA Management Consultancy Study	£75,000	DTI
IAEA Technical Assistance and Co-operation Fund	£2,504,581	DTI
IAEA UK Transport Safety Appraisal	£31,702	DTI
International Telecommunication Union	£2,007,257	DTI
Nuclear Security Fund	£250,000	DTI
Contribution under UK Safeguards Support Programme	£105,000	DTI
T&S for IAEA personnel associated with UNSP	£55,000	DTI
Birdekin National Institutions	£150,000	FCO
Support for International Criminal Tribunals/ICC	£350,000	FCO
The Hague Academy for International Law	£7,000	FCO
UN Centre for International Crime Prevention	£210,000	FCO
UN Global Compact	£57,000	FCO
UN Office (OHCHR) in Colombia	£120,000	FCO
UN Office of Internal Oversight Services Trust Fund	£13,666	FCO
UN Special Rapporteur on Disabilities	£10,000	FCO
UN Voluntary Fund for Technical Co-operation	£100,000	FCO
Sierra Leone Special Court	£650,000	FCO
UN Voluntary Fund for the Victims of Torture	£175,000	FCO
UN Weapons Convention	£23,337	FCO
UN International Drug Control Programme	£4,066,722	CO/HO/ DFID
World Meteorological Organisation	£612,000	MET OFFICE

TOTAL   **£386,097,270**

**TOTAL OF ASSESSED AND
VOLUNTARY CONTRIBUTIONS**   **£590,349,163**

2. UK PERSONNEL WORKING ON THE UNITED NATIONS

	Posted from the UK	Locally Employed
UK Mission to the UN in New York	41	34
UK Mission to the UN in Geneva	20	1
UK Mission to the UN in Vienna	8	0
UK Mission to the UN in Nairobi	1	1
United Nations Department, FCO	40	–

(Note: This only lists the main Departments and posts. There are many other people in the FCO, other Government Departments and posts abroad who work full or part time on issues connected with the United Nations).

Printed in the UK by The Stationery Office Limited
on behalf of the Controller of Her Majesty's Stationery Office
09/03, 19585, 153358

ISBN 0-10-158982-4

Published by TSO (The Stationery Office) and available from:

Online
www.tso.co.uk/bookshop

Mail, Telephone, Fax & E-mail
TSO
PO Box 29, Norwich NR3 1GN
Telephone orders/General enquiries 0870 600 5522
Order through the Parliamentary Hotline *Lo-Call* 0845 7 023474
Fax orders 0870 600 5533
Email book.orders@tso.co.uk
Textphone 0870 240 3701

TSO Shops
123 Kingsway, London WC2B 6PQ
020 7242 6393 Fax 020 7242 6394
68-69 Bull Street, Birmingham B4 6AD
0121 236 9696 Fax 0121 236 9699
9-21 Princess Street, Manchester M60 8AS
0161 834 7201 Fax 0161 833 0634
16 Arthur Street, Belfast BT1 4GD
028 9023 8451 Fax 028 9023 5401
18-19 High Street, Cardiff CF10 1PT
029 2039 5548 Fax 029 2038 4347
71 Lothian Road, Edinburgh EH3 9AZ
0870 606 5566 Fax 0870 606 5588

TSO Accredited Agents
(See Yellow Pages)

and through good booksellers